Collins

Science

KS3 Revision

Science

KS3

Year 9
Workbook

Francesca Walsh
Dan Evans
Ron Holt

0 — 1000ml
APPROX.

100 — 900

800

700

600

500

400

300

Ex20°C
100ml ± 1ml

0   100

10   90

20   80

30   70

40   60

50

40

30

20

10

Contents

Biology

Chemistry

Physics

Answers

Acknowledgements

p7 © Shutterstock.com/Lucie Lang; p11 © Shutterstock.com/bahri altay; p14 © Shutterstock.com/ leungchopan; p25 © Shutterstock.com/grebcha, © Shutterstock.com/ leafen.com, © Shutterstock.com/ Andre Adams; p26 © Shutterstock.com/RTimages; p27 © Shutterstock.com/Sherry Yates Young; p38 © ChameleonsEye/Shutterstock.com; p38 © Jorg Hackemann/Shutterstock.com; p39 © standa_art/ Shutterstock.com; p43 © Webspark/Shutterstock.com; p44 © photoiconix/Shutterstock.com; p46 © LiudmilaKorsakova/Shutterstock.com; p46 © whitehoune/Shutterstock.com; p48 © guentermanaus/ Shutterstock.com; p49 © pzAxe/Shutterstock.com; p68 © Shutterstock.com/ Flashon Studio; p69 © Zern Liew/Shutterstock.com

Vocabulary Builder

1 Choose words from the box to fit the descriptions below.
You may use the words more than once.

variation	gametes	clone	chromosome
mutation	species	gene	

a) A strand of DNA that contains genes .... [1]

b) Male and female sex cells .... [1]

c) Humans have 23 pairs of these .... [1]

d) A section of DNA that controls a characteristic .... [1]

e) A group of similar organisms that can reproduce
with each other to give fertile offspring .... [1]

f) Differences in organisms of the same or
different species .... [1]

g) A change in the DNA sequence, often caused by
an error in DNA replication .... [1]

h) An organism for which all genetic material
comes from one parent .... [1]

2 The following passage is about sexual reproduction.
Fill in the missing words. The first letter of each word has been given.

When animals reproduce sexually, two **g** .... join together. This process

is called **f** .... The offspring will contain **g** ....

i .... from both parents and the offspring will **i** ....

characteristics from both parents. [4]

3 Fossils provide evidence of animals that lived millions of years ago but are no longer living.
What term we do we use to describe such animals?

.... [1]

4 Complete the following passage by circling the most appropriate words in bold.

Inside the **cytoplasm / nucleus** of a human body cell there are **23 / 46** chromosomes. The chromosomes are made of **DNA / RNA**.

Genes / Characteristics are located on the chromosomes and are responsible for inherited features. When a body cell divides, the **parent / daughter** cells receive an exact copy of all the chromosomes in the **parent / daughter** cell. [6]

5 What is a **monoculture**?

.... [1]

Total Marks .... / 20

Maths Skills

1 The graph below shows the different blood groups within a population.

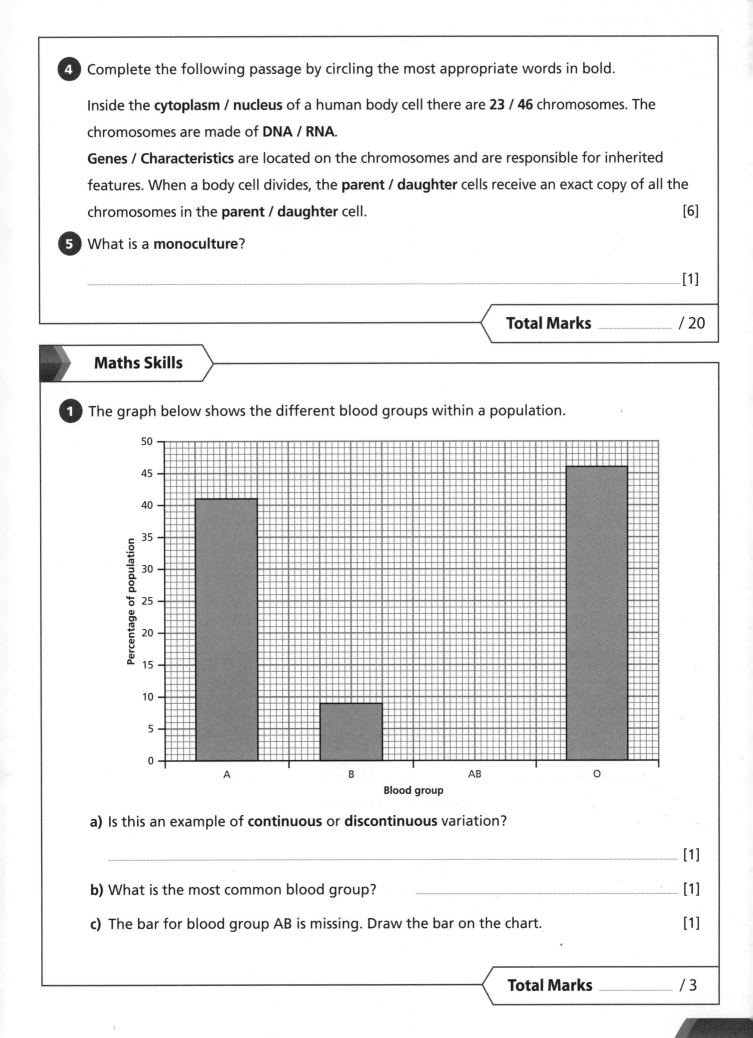

a) Is this an example of **continuous** or **discontinuous** variation?

.... [1]

b) What is the most common blood group? .... [1]

c) The bar for blood group AB is missing. Draw the bar on the chart. [1]

Total Marks .... / 3

1 For each of the human characteristics below, decide whether they are examples of **continuous** or **discontinuous** variation by placing them in the correct column in the table.

| height | size of feet | eye colour | ear lobe shape |
| weight | right- or left-handed | | ability to roll tongue |

Continuous	Discontinuous

[7]

2 A farmer notices that the potatoes in his harvest show variation in size.
Name three environmental factors that could be responsible for this variation.

....

....[3]

3 Tom grows tomato plants.
Suggest three characteristics that genes may control in the tomatoes.

....

....[3]

4 Julie says that many characteristics in humans vary due to both genetic and environmental variation.
Explain what she means, using height as an example.

....

....

....

....[2]

5 a) Explain how natural selection takes place.

....

....

....

.... [4]

b) Which two scientists developed the **Theory of Natural Selection**?

.... and .... [2]

6 Normal Leopard Geckos are a dull yellow colour with black spots. Albino Leopard Geckos lack black pigment in their skin so have no spots. Whether a gecko is Normal Leopard or Albino Leopard is inherited. The allele for albino colouring is recessive.

The Punnett square below shows a cross between two geckos.

Male lizard

	A	A
a	Aa	Aa
a	Aa	Aa

Female lizard

Key: A = Normal Leopard

a = Albino Leopard

a) Is the male gecko Normal Leopard or Albino Leopard in appearance?

.... [1]

b) Is the female gecko Normal Leopard or Albino Leopard in appearance?

.... [1]

c) Are the offspring Normal Leopard or Albino Leopard in appearance?

.... [1]

d) If two of the offspring were bred together, what would be the expected ratio of Normal Leopard to Albino Leopard geckos?

.... [1]

7 **a)** On the diagram below, fill in the missing chromosome numbers for a human.

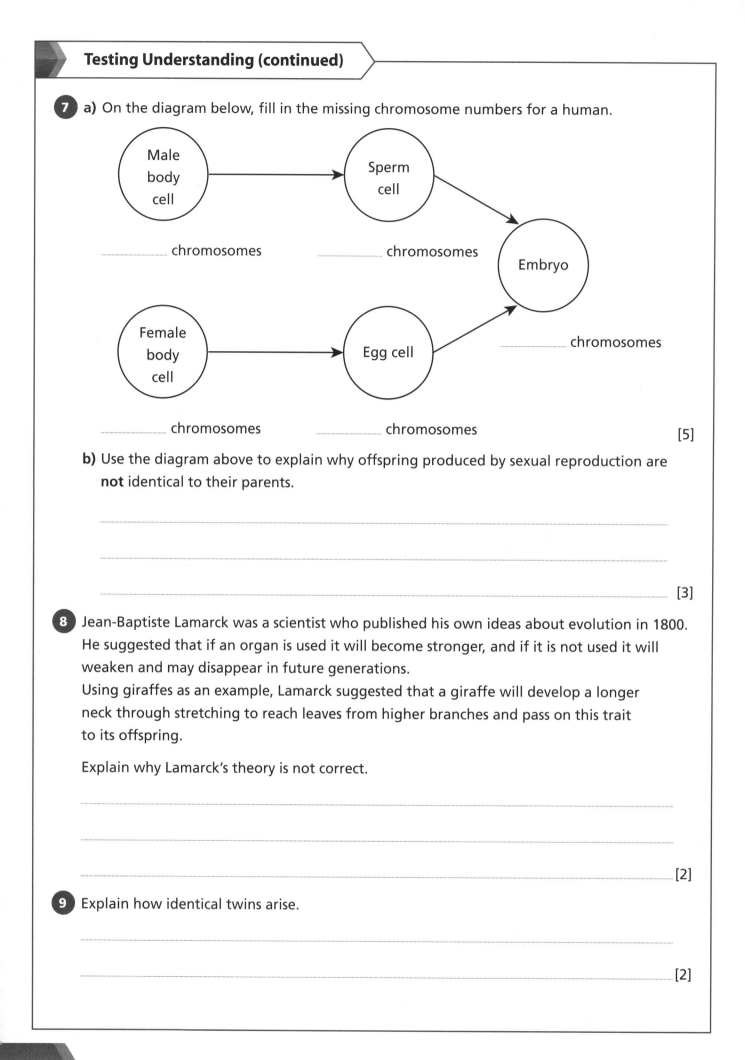

_____ chromosomes

_____ chromosomes

_____ chromosomes

_____ chromosomes

_____ chromosomes

[5]

b) Use the diagram above to explain why offspring produced by sexual reproduction are **not** identical to their parents.

....

....

....

....

[3]

8 Jean-Baptiste Lamarck was a scientist who published his own ideas about evolution in 1800. He suggested that if an organ is used it will become stronger, and if it is not used it will weaken and may disappear in future generations.

Using giraffes as an example, Lamarck suggested that a giraffe will develop a longer neck through stretching to reach leaves from higher branches and pass on this trait to its offspring.

Explain why Lamarck's theory is not correct.

....

....

....

[2]

9 Explain how identical twins arise.

....

....

[2]

10 Underline the features below that may be affected by the physical environment in which a tomato plant grows.

A: How large the leaves grow   B: The shape of the leaves

C: How tall the plant grows   D: The shape of the petals

E: The perfume of the flower   F: The size of the fruit   [3]

11 Underline the statements below that are true for **asexual** reproduction.

A: Requires only one parent   B: Provides for genetic variation in offspring

C: Only happens in animals   D: Requires two gametes

E: Offspring are identical to parent   [2]

12 Garden peas can produce either smooth or wrinkled seeds.

a) Is this an example of **continuous** or **discontinuous** variation?

.... [1]

b) In peas, the smooth seed is dominant.
   What does the term **dominant** mean?

....

.... [2]

c) Milena says that it is possible to get wrinkled seeds even if both parent plants have smooth seeds.
   Is she correct? Explain your answer by drawing a Punnett square in the space below.

   Yes / No   [2]

d) In 1865, following eight years of research on over 10 000 pea plants, Mendel published his ideas on **Laws of Inheritance**.
   Explain why his ideas were not accepted at that time.

....

.... [2]

13 Species such as the dodo and the triceratops became extinct many years ago.
Suggest two causes for the extinction of a species.

....

.... [2]

14 What do you understand by the term **selective breeding**?

....

....

.... [3]

15 Which of the following statements about **cloning** are true (**T**) and which are false (**F**)?
Write **T** or **F** in the spaces provided.

a) Clones always have the same genetic information as each other. .... [1]

b) Clones are always genetically identical to the host mother. .... [1]

c) Plants cannot be cloned. .... [1]

d) Cloning is a type of asexual reproduction. .... [1]

e) One embryo can be used to produce many clones. .... [1]

f) Clones can happen naturally in plants. .... [1]

16 Dolly the sheep was the first mammal to be cloned from an adult cell.
The stages below outline how Dolly was produced, but they are in the wrong order.
Use numbers **1–5** to place them in the correct order.
The first one has been done for you.

Remove the nucleus from the egg cell. ☐

Insert the nucleus from the body cell into the empty egg cell. ☐

Remove an egg cell from an adult female sheep. ⬚ 1

Place the new egg cell into a donor sheep. ☐

Remove the nucleus from a body cell from a different sheep. ☐ [2]

17 DNA can be extracted from living cells and used for a number of applications. Suggest two applications of DNA extraction.

....

.... [2]

18 The diagram below represents a molecule found inside cells.

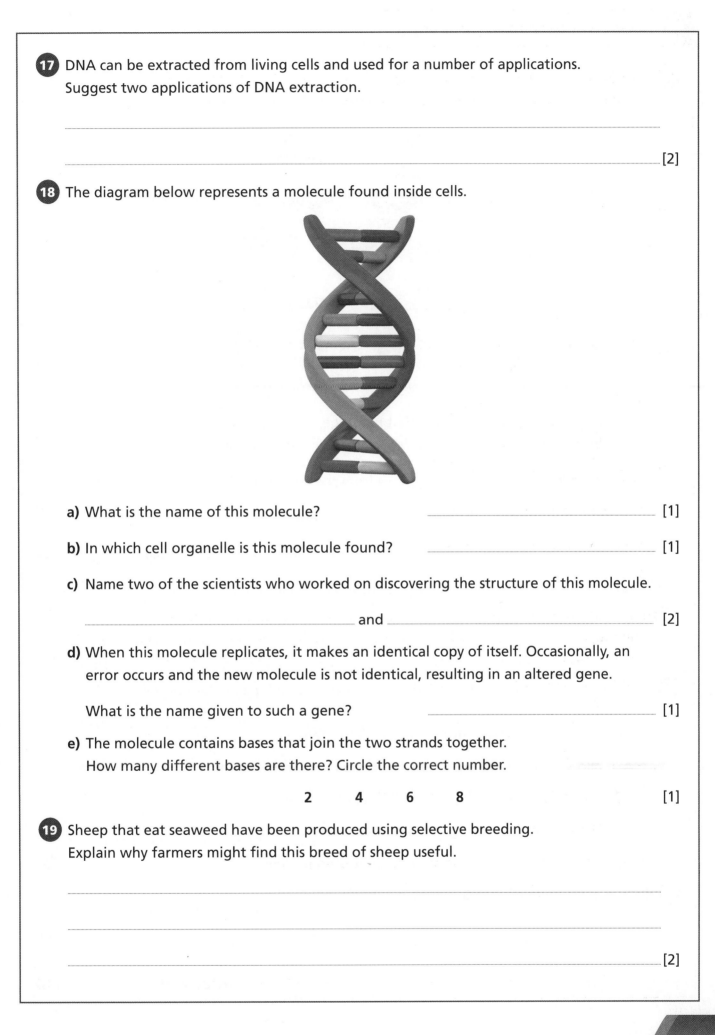

a) What is the name of this molecule? .... [1]

b) In which cell organelle is this molecule found? .... [1]

c) Name two of the scientists who worked on discovering the structure of this molecule.

.... and .... [2]

d) When this molecule replicates, it makes an identical copy of itself. Occasionally, an error occurs and the new molecule is not identical, resulting in an altered gene.

What is the name given to such a gene? .... [1]

e) The molecule contains bases that join the two strands together.
How many different bases are there? Circle the correct number.

2   4   6   8 [1]

19 Sheep that eat seaweed have been produced using selective breeding. Explain why farmers might find this breed of sheep useful.

....

....

.... [2]

20 Dinesh has two different tomato plants.
Plant A has large, yellow tomatoes. Plant B has small, red tomatoes.

Large, yellow tomato →   ← Small, red tomato

A   B

a) Dinesh wants to produce a plant that has large, red tomatoes.
Complete the instructions below to explain what Dinesh must do.

i) Collect some _____ from the anthers of plant B. [1]

ii) Place this on the _____ of plant A. [1]

iii) Collect the _____ from the tomatoes that grow on plant A. [1]

iv) _____ the seeds he has collected into soil. [1]

b) What is the name given to the process above?

_____ [1]

21 In the 18th century, a scientist called Carl Linnaeus started the modern system
of classification.
Underline the reasons why such a system is important.

A: It allows us to group organisms by observing typical features

B: It allows us to group organisms by where they live

C: It allows us to predict organisms at risk of extinction

D: It helps us to clarify the relationship between organisms [2]

22 Give two examples of natural clones in plants.

_____ and _____ [2]

Total Marks _____ / 82

1 Read the passage below about peppered moths and then answer the questions that follow.

Until the early 1800s, peppered moths always had pale, speckled wings. However, in 1845, a moth with dark grey wings was found. Over the next ten years, the number of grey moths increased, whilst the number of moths with pale wings decreased. A scientist called Kettlewell thought this change in numbers was because pollution from factories was causing the bark on the trees to turn grey and the dark moths were better adapted to living on these trees.

Kettlewell tested his idea by releasing equal numbers of pale and grey moths into two forests. The first forest in Birmingham was heavily affected by pollution; the second forest in Dorset was not affected by pollution. Kettlewell set up traps to capture and count the moths several months later. In Dorset, twice as many pale moths as dark moths were recaptured. In Birmingham, twice as many dark moths were recaptured.

a) What is the most likely reason for the appearance of the first grey moth in 1845?

.... [1]

b) Suggest why Kettlewell thought that dark moths would be better adapted to living on trees with grey bark.

.... [1]

c) Suggest one factor that Kettlewell should have tried to control in his experiment.

.... [1]

d) Suggest one factor that he would have been unable to control.

.... [1]

e) Underline the two statements below that are valid conclusions from Kettlewell's experiment.

   A: More dark moths than pale moths survived in the Birmingham forest.

   B: More dark moths were eaten in the Dorset forest.

   C: There was more food available for the pale moths in the Dorset forest.

   D: Pale moths do not survive as well as dark moths in forests exposed to pollution.   [2]

Total Marks .... / 6

1 Read the passage below about the conservation of endangered species and then answer the questions that follow.

It is estimated that within the next 50 years, 30 per cent of all animals will become **extinct** as a result of massive **growth in human population**, which has led to **habitat destruction**.

In 1996, the Frozen Ark project was set up as a **gene bank** to save samples of frozen cells containing the **DNA** of endangered animals. Cells can be collected from samples such as mouth swabs, hairs, feathers, blood and faeces. They are frozen to very low temperatures and can then be stored safely for hundreds of years. These samples take up very little space and can be used in the future to produce whole animals from the cells using processes such as **cloning**. The frozen samples can also be used to help animals currently endangered by increasing **genetic variation** within their populations.

Captive breeding programmes have also been used for many years to preserve and increase numbers of endangered species. Edinburgh Zoo announced in August 2013 that a giant panda in their captive breeding programme was pregnant; however, two months later, the zoo reported that the panda had lost her baby. A spokesperson from the zoo said, 'It often takes three or four attempts for a captive panda to produce young.'

a) What does the term **endangered** mean?

_____ [1]

b) Suggest two ways that habitats have been destroyed.

_____ and _____ [2]

c) How do captive breeding programmes differ from gene banks?

_____

_____ [2]

d) Suggest one advantage that gene banks have over captive breeding programmes.

_____ [1]

e) Why is it important to increase genetic variation in a population?

_____

_____

_____ [2]

2 The table below gives information about two animals that were successfully cloned in the year 2000.

Type of Animal	Mouflon sheep	Domestic pig
Number of Embryos	7 embryos implanted in 4 female sheep	401 embryos implanted in 7 female pigs
Number of Pregnancies	2 pregnancies	1 pregnancy
Number of Live Births	1 birth	5 births
Reason for Cloning	The mouflon sheep are an endangered species	The company hoped to use the pigs to grow organs that could be used for human transplants
Where Cells to be Cloned Came From	The sheep was created from cells from a sheep found dead at a wildlife rescue centre in Italy	A pig that had successfully provided cells for human transplants

a) For which animal did cloning have the highest success rate in providing a live birth compared to the number of embryos implanted? Explain your answer.

....

.... [2]

b) Suggest reasons **for** and **against** the cloning of pigs in the example above.

For: ....

....

Against: ....

.... [2]

c) Suggest a **disadvantage** of using cloning for species that are endangered.

.... [1]

Total Marks .... / 13

	Vocabulary Builder	Maths Skills	Testing Understanding	Working Scientifically	Science in Use
Total Marks	.... / 20	.... / 3	.... / 82	.... / 6	.... / 13

Vocabulary Builder

1 Choose words from the box that the sentences below are describing.

anaemia	stimulant	antibiotic	toxin
nicotine	recreational	carcinogen	

a) The name given to a drug not used for medical reasons .... [1]

b) An addictive substance found in cigarettes .... [1]

c) A condition caused by a lack of iron .... [1]

d) A drug that speeds up body systems .... [1]

e) A chemical that can cause cancer .... [1]

f) A drug used to treat bacterial infections .... [1]

g) A poisonous substance produced by bacteria
and viruses .... [1]

2 Complete the passage below about bacteria by circling the correct words in bold.

Bacteria are **single-celled / multicellular** organisms. They do not have a **nucleus / cell wall**. The genetic material lies freely within the **mitochondria / cytoplasm**. Bacteria that cause disease are called **mutagens / pathogens**. Bacterial infections can be treated with **antibiotics / analgesics**. Sometimes bacteria develop **immunity / resistance** to drugs. This happens when bacteria **reproduce / mutate** to produce a new strain. [7]

3 Complete the sentences below by filling in the missing words.

a) Red blood cells carry .... [1]

b) White blood cells produce .... , which help fight disease. [1]

c) Platelets help the blood to .... [1]

d) Drugs that are effective in treating viral infections are called .... [1]

e) Blood cells are produced in the .... [1]

f) Cirrhosis is a disease that affects the .... [1]

4 In each of the following lists, circle the **odd one out**. Give a reason for each answer.

a) measles   mumps   cholera   chickenpox

Reason: .... [2]

b) aspirin   cocaine   caffeine   alcohol

Reason: .... [2]

c) bacteria   lymphocyte   fungus   virus

Reason: .... [2]

5 What does the term **addiction** mean?

....

.... [2]

6 Circle the words in bold that make the sentences below correct.

a) An unwanted effect of a drug is called a **symptom / side effect**.   [1]

b) In the respiratory system, **cilia / goblet cells** trap dust and particles.   [1]

c) Ecstasy and cocaine are examples of **class A / class B** drugs.   [1]

d) Influenza and chickenpox are examples of **non-infectious / infectious** diseases.   [1]

e) **Bacteria / Viruses** can only reproduce inside living cells.   [1]

7 Explain the difference between first and second line defence systems in the body.

....

....

....

.... [5]

8 The following passage is about vaccines.
Fill in the missing words. The first letter of each word has been given.

A vaccine is a **w** .... or dead form of the microbe that causes the disease.

Vaccines bring about an **i** .... **r** .... in the body.

W .... blood cells produce **a** ...., which destroy the

microbe. They also produce **m** .... **c** ...., which will

recognise the microbe if it is encountered again.   [5]

Total Marks .... / 43

1 The graph below shows the number of bacteria in a sample of milk that was placed at 15°C.

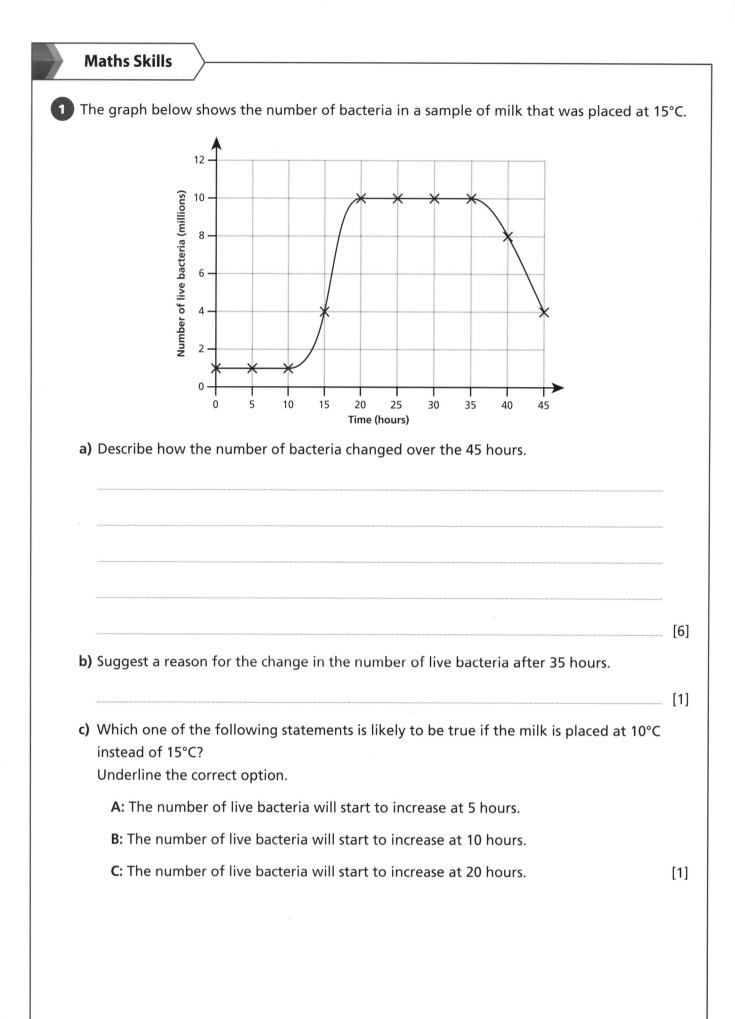

a) Describe how the number of bacteria changed over the 45 hours.

....

....

....

....

....

.... [6]

b) Suggest a reason for the change in the number of live bacteria after 35 hours.

.... [1]

c) Which one of the following statements is likely to be true if the milk is placed at 10°C instead of 15°C?
Underline the correct option.

   A: The number of live bacteria will start to increase at 5 hours.

   B: The number of live bacteria will start to increase at 10 hours.

   C: The number of live bacteria will start to increase at 20 hours. [1]

2 The two graphs below show antibody levels in a person.

Chart A shows how levels change following initial vaccination against a pathogen.

Chart B shows how levels change when they are exposed to the same pathogen several years later.

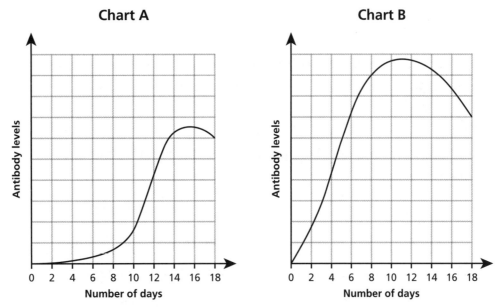

Chart A   Chart B

a) Describe two ways in which antibody production differs following initial vaccination and exposure following vaccination.

....

.... [2]

b) A recent study carried out in the UK found that 90% of children had received the MMR vaccination by the age of three, whilst 3% had been vaccinated against measles only. 7% of children had received neither vaccination.

Show this information on the pie chart below.

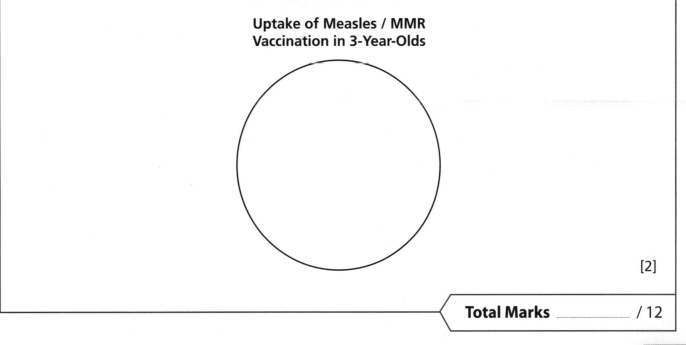

**Uptake of Measles / MMR
Vaccination in 3-Year-Olds**

[2]

Total Marks .... / 12

1 Alcohol is absorbed into the body through the stomach and the small intestine.

a) Give the name of one organ that is damaged by drinking a lot of alcohol over a long period of time.

_____ [1]

b) If a pregnant woman drinks alcohol, the alcohol may pass into the foetus. Name the organ through which the alcohol passes into the foetus.

_____ [1]

c) Which of the following are short-term effects of alcohol on the body? Circle the correct options.

memory loss	**brain damage**
mouth cancer	**decreased coordination**

[2]

2 Match each disease to its cause by drawing a line between the two.

Disease	Cause
Down's syndrome	Vitamin C deficiency
Cholera	Virus
Chickenpox	Genetically inherited
Scurvy	Bacteria

[3]

3 Some people feel that cannabis should be made legal because it can provide pain relief for people suffering from a number of medical conditions.

a) Give one medical condition for which cannabis can be beneficial in providing pain relief.

_____ [1]

b) Give two possible harmful effects on the body of using cannabis.

_____

_____ [2]

4 Cigarettes contain many harmful substances, including **tar**, **nicotine** and **carbon monoxide**. For each of the statements below, decide which one of these substances it relates to.

a) Causes high blood pressure .... [1]

b) Coats the lining of the lungs .... [1]

c) Contains carcinogens .... [1]

d) Is a poisonous gas .... [1]

e) Is taken up by red blood cells .... [1]

5 a) The drugs in the box below are either **legal** or **illegal**.
Write each one in the correct column in the table.

aspirin	antibiotics
cannabis	speed
caffeine	ecstasy

Legal	Illegal

[6]

b) People who are addicted to a drug may experience a number of symptoms when they stop taking that drug, such as nausea, headaches, sweating and insomnia.

What term describes such symptoms? .... [1]

6 What are the three ways in which white blood cells help to defend the body?

....

....

....
[3]

7 Which of the following statements are true (**T**) and which are false (**F**)?
Write **T** or **F** in the spaces provided.

a) Red blood cells produce antibodies. .... [1]

b) Blood cells are produced in the bone marrow. .... [1]

c) Antibiotics can be used to treat bacterial infections. .... [1]

d) Viruses are larger than bacteria. .... [1]

e) Vaccinations cannot be used to protect against viral diseases. .... [1]

f) Phagocytes produce toxins. .... [1]

8 **a)** Which component of the blood helps in the formation of a scab?

_____ [1]

b) Why is scab formation classed as a 'first line of defence'?

_____ [1]

9 The following statements outline how the measles vaccination works, but they are in the wrong order.
Number the statements **1–8** to show the correct order.
The first and last ones have been done for you.

The memory cells produce large quantities of antibodies rapidly. ☐

White blood cells detect the measles antigen. ☐

The person catches measles. ☐

A person is injected with measles antigen. ☐ **1**

The memory cells recognise the antigen. ☐

The antibodies destroy the measles virus. ☐ **8**

White blood cells produce antibodies and also form memory cells. ☐

The memory cells reproduce rapidly. ☐ [3]

10 Explain how each of the following helps to defend the body against infection.

a) Acid in the stomach

_____ [1]

b) Mucus and cilia in the respiratory system

_____

_____ [2]

c) The skin

_____ [1]

d) Tears

_____ [1]

11 Which of the following do all pathogenic bacteria need to grow? Circle the correct options.

warmth   oxygen   acid   moisture   food   light   [3]

12 Decide whether the diseases below are caused by a **bacteria**, **fungus** or **virus**.
Write them in the correct column in the table.

| chickenpox | tuberculosis | salmonella food poisoning | mumps |
| influenza | measles | athlete's foot | cholera |

Bacteria	Fungus	Virus

[8]

13 Draw a line from each named drug to the group in which it belongs.

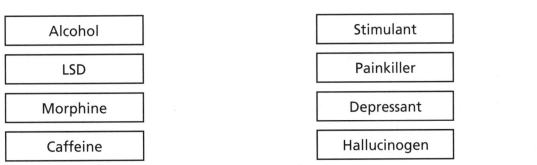

Drug		**Group**
Alcohol		Stimulant
LSD		Painkiller
Morphine		Depressant
Caffeine		Hallucinogen

[3]

14 Withdrawal symptoms occur when someone stops taking a drug they are addicted to.
Put each of the symptoms from the box below into the correct column in the table to show
whether it is an **emotional** or a **physical** symptom.

| vomiting | anxiety | diarrhoea |
| insomnia | depression | shaking |

Emotional Symptom	Physical Symptom

[6]

15 Explain why people who smoke cigarettes often find themselves short of breath when exercising.

....

....

....

.... [6]

16 Microbial diseases can be spread in a number of ways.

a) Match the diseases below to their method of spread by drawing lines between them.

Disease	How it is Spread
Malaria	Air
HIV	Blood / bodily fluids
Cholera	Animals
Colds	Water / food

[3]

b) How do hospitals minimise the spread of disease from one patient to another?

....

.... [3]

17 a) MRSA (methicillin-resistant *Staphylococcus aureus*) is a superbug.
What is a superbug?

....

.... [2]

b) Explain how a superbug develops.

....

....

....

.... [4]

c) *Staphylococcus* is a round-shaped bacterium.
   Name one other shape that bacteria may be.

   .... [1]

Total Marks .... / 80

1 Hope has a sample of milk that has turned sour. She wants to find out whether there are any bacteria in it. She decides to put some of the milk onto a Petri dish containing agar and uses the equipment shown below.

Bunsen Burner   **Petri Dish with Agar**   **A**

a) Hope uses the tool labelled **A** to put some milk onto the agar in the Petri dish.
   What is the name of this piece of equipment? Circle the correct option.

   inoculating needle   **inoculating iron**   **inoculating loop**   [1]

b) Hope heats tool **A** in the Bunsen burner before she dips it into the milk.
   Explain why she does this.

   .... [1]

c) After Hope has placed some milk onto the agar, she seals the Petri dish with sticky tape.
   Explain why she does this.

   ....

   .... [1]

d) Hope places the Petri dish in an incubator for the bacteria to grow.
   What temperature should she use to incubate the Petri dish? Circle the correct option.

   10°C   **25°C**   **42°C**   **55°C**   [1]

e) For how long should Hope leave the Petri dish in the incubator? Circle the correct option.

   10–20 minutes   **5–10 hours**   **1–2 days**   **1–2 weeks**   [1]

2 Wayne and Rosie want to investigate how drinking coffee affects heart rate. They decide that Wayne will drink some coffee and Rosie will drink the same amount of water. They will then each measure their heart rate to see which is higher.

a) Give one reason why their method will not provide valid results.

_____ [1]

b) What is the **independent** variable in this experiment?

_____ [1]

c) What is the **dependent** variable?

_____ [1]

d) How can Wayne measure his heart rate?

_____ [1]

e) The coffee contains caffeine.
What would you expect to happen to Wayne's heart rate?

_____ [1]

3 Some students wanted to look at blood cells under a microscope. They placed some blood onto a piece of glass.

a) What is the name of the piece of glass on which the blood has been placed?

_____ [1]

b) On which part of the microscope is the glass placed?

_____ [1]

c) The drawing shows one of the cells that the students see.
What is the name of this cell?

_____ [1]

Total Marks _____ / 13

1 Read the passage below about flu and then answer the questions that follow.

Flu can be unpleasant, but if you are otherwise healthy it will usually clear up on its own within a week. **Antiviral medicine** can lessen the symptoms of flu and shorten its duration, but **antibiotics are of no use**.

However, flu can be more severe in certain **risk groups** and it is recommended that people in these groups have a **flu vaccine**. Over time, protection from the injected flu vaccine gradually decreases and flu strains often change. So, new flu vaccines are produced each year, which is why people advised to have the flu jab need it every year.

When flu is spreading widely, apart from vaccination, **hygiene** is the only other method that can help prevent it spreading further. In January 2011, the government launched a campaign to reduce spread of the flu virus. The 'Catch it, Bin it, Kill it' campaign recommended people carry tissues to catch coughs and sneezes, dispose of the tissue as soon as possible and then kill germs as soon as possible by washing their hands.

a) Suggest two ways that the flu virus is likely to be spread.

....

.... [2]

b) Why are antibiotics of no use in the treatment of flu?

....

.... [2]

c) Give an example of a person who may fall into an **at risk** group

.... [1]

d) A person who has been vaccinated against flu may continue to have antibodies against the virus in their blood a year later, but may still catch flu. Explain why.

....

.... [2]

Total Marks .... / 7

	Vocabulary Builder	Maths Skills	Testing Understanding	Working Scientifically	Science in Use
Total Marks	.... / 43	.... / 12	.... / 80	.... / 13	.... / 7

Chemistry — Obtaining Useful Materials

Vocabulary Builder

1 What name is given to rocks from which metals can be economically obtained? Underline the correct option.

   A: Minerals   B: Ores

   C: Igneous rocks   D: Aggregates   [1]

2 Draw lines to match each material to the correct description of how it is formed.

Type of Material   **Formation**

| Ceramics |
| Polymers |
| Composites |

Formed by combining two different materials that often have very different properties

Formed by the heating and subsequent cooling of an inorganic material, e.g. clay

Formed by joining together lots of small molecules   [2]

3 When calcium carbonate is heated, it forms calcium oxide and carbon dioxide. What type of reaction is this? Underline the correct option.

   A: Oxidation   B: Reduction

   C: Thermal decomposition   D: Combustion   [1]

4 Underline the type of reaction occurring when a more reactive metal takes the place of a less reactive metal in a compound. An example is shown in the word equation below.

Zinc + Copper oxide → Zinc oxide + Copper

   A: Combustion   B: Thermal decomposition

   C: Displacement   D: Neutralisation   [1]

5 Fill in the missing words below to identify the different types of reaction being defined.

   a) When oxygen is lost from a compound, a _____ reaction has occurred. [1]

   b) Reactions that absorb heat from the surroundings are called _____ reactions.   [1]

   c) When the temperature increases during a reaction, an _____ reaction has occurred.   [1]

Total Marks _____ / 8

1 The metal aluminium is extracted from its ore, called bauxite.

After mining, the metal is extracted from the ore before being sold.

The table below shows the mining and extraction costs and the selling costs in two different fictional countries, Oreland and Mineralstan.

Country	Cost of Mining One Tonne of Bauxite (£)	Cost of Extracting Aluminium from One Tonne of Bauxite (£)	Selling Price of One Tonne of Aluminium (£)
Oreland	50	100	200
Mineralstan	70	120	200

a) What is the **total** cost of obtaining one tonne of aluminium in each country?

Oreland: ~~£350~~ 150 [1]

Mineralstan: £ ~~390~~ 190 [1]

b) In which country is the production of aluminium more profitable?
Explain your answer.

Oreland as the cost of obtaining and selling the aluminium is cheaper which means more can [3] be sold and bought whilst in mineralstan the high costs prevent lots of selling

c) If mining costs increase by 50%, how much profit will be made in Oreland per tonne of aluminium?
Show your working.

200 = 50%   200 x2 = 400 = 100%
Cost of obtaining (metal) = 150
400 - 150 = 250   so profit = £25 [3] 0

d) If the cost of extracting aluminium doubles but the selling price of aluminium stays the same, do you think Oreland will still produce aluminium?
Explain your answer.

No   as Oreland would start loosing money pur sell sold pound and would make no profit as [2] the product extraction would cost £300 and it would be sold for 200 meaning oreland would loose £100 per pound sold.

2 Copper can be obtained from copper oxide by passing methane gas over heated copper oxide. The diagram below shows how this experiment can be carried out. The boiling tube has a hole at one end so the unused methane can escape and be burnt.

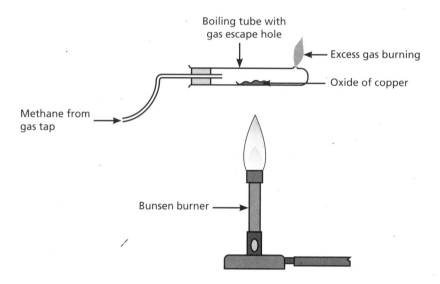

Kumar carried out this experiment. His results table is shown below.

Mass of Empty Boiling Tube	20.45g
Mass of Boiling Tube and Copper Oxide Powder	23.65g
Mass of Boiling Tube and Copper at End of Experiment	23.01g

a) What mass of copper oxide powder did Kumar use?
   Show your working.

   .... [2]

b) What mass of copper remained at the end of the reaction?
   Show your working.

   .... [2]

c) What mass of oxygen was present in the original copper oxide?
   Show your working.

   .... [2]

d) Using your answers to parts a) and b), calculate the percentage (by mass) of copper in copper oxide.
   Show your working.

   ....

   .... [2]

Total Marks .... / 18

1 A reactivity series of metals is shown on the right.

a) What does the reactivity series show?

_____

_____ [1]

b) Why are elements such as potassium **not** found in the Earth's crust as the pure metal?

_____

_____ [1]

Potassium
Sodium
Calcium
Magnesium
Aluminium
Zinc
Iron
Copper
Gold

c) Metals can be extracted from their oxides by heating the metal oxide with a more reactive metal.

Name a metal from the reactivity series that can be used to extract magnesium from magnesium oxide.

_____ [1]

d) Consider the two equations below. X is a metal.

X + Copper oxide → X oxide + Copper

X + Iron oxide → No reaction

Where should metal X be placed in the reactivity series?
Explain your answer.

_____

_____

_____

_____ [3]

e) Will potassium carbonate decompose at a higher or lower temperature than zinc carbonate?
Explain your answer.

_____

_____

_____ [2]

2 A few metals (for example, gold) are found in the Earth's crust as the pure metal. Some metals can be extracted from their ores by heating the ore with carbon. For example, the ore galena contains the compound lead sulfide (PbS). After roasting (heating with oxygen), galena is turned into lead oxide. The lead can be extracted by heating with carbon, as shown in the equation below.

$$2PbO + C \rightarrow 2Pb + CO_2$$

a) Why are metals such as gold found as the pure metal?

.... [1]

b) What is meant by the term **ore**?

....

....

.... [2]

c) How are ores usually obtained from the Earth?

.... [1]

d) In the above equation, which substance has been reduced?
Explain your answer.

....

.... [2]

e) The reaction above is a **displacement reaction**.
Explain why.

....

....

.... [2]

f) If copper was used instead of carbon, the reaction would not occur.
Explain why.

....

.... [2]

g) Other metals, such as magnesium, can be used instead of carbon to extract lead from lead oxide.

Suggest why magnesium is not used.

....

....

.... [2]

h) The diagram below represents the arrangement of atoms in lead oxide and in carbon.

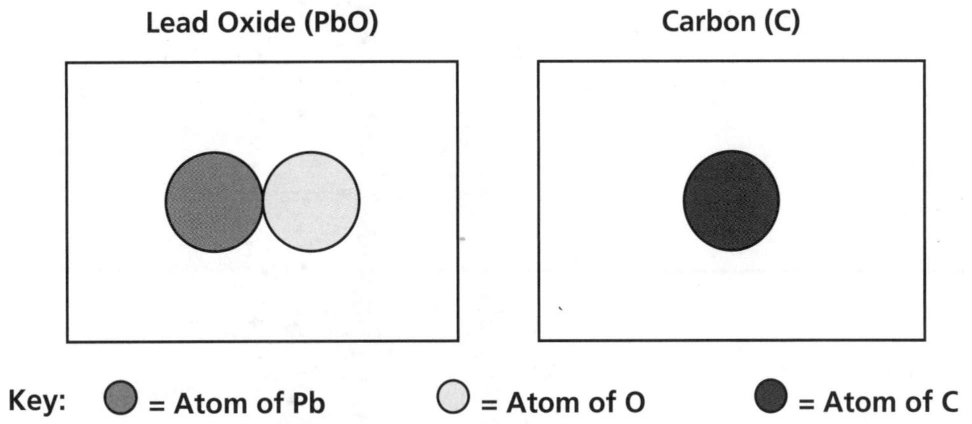

Lead Oxide (PbO)   **Carbon (C)**

Key: ◐ = Atom of Pb   ○ = Atom of O   ● = Atom of C

In the boxes below, draw diagrams to represent the arrangement of atoms in lead and carbon dioxide.

Lead   **Carbon Dioxide**

[2]

3 Which of the following statements about the properties of ceramics are true (**T**) and which are false (**F**)?
Write **T** or **F** in the spaces provided.

a) Ceramics are hard. .... [1]

b) Ceramics retain their strength at high temperatures. .... [1]

c) Ceramics are malleable. .... [1]

d) Ceramics are resistant to wear. .... [1]

④ A diagram of a blast furnace is shown below.

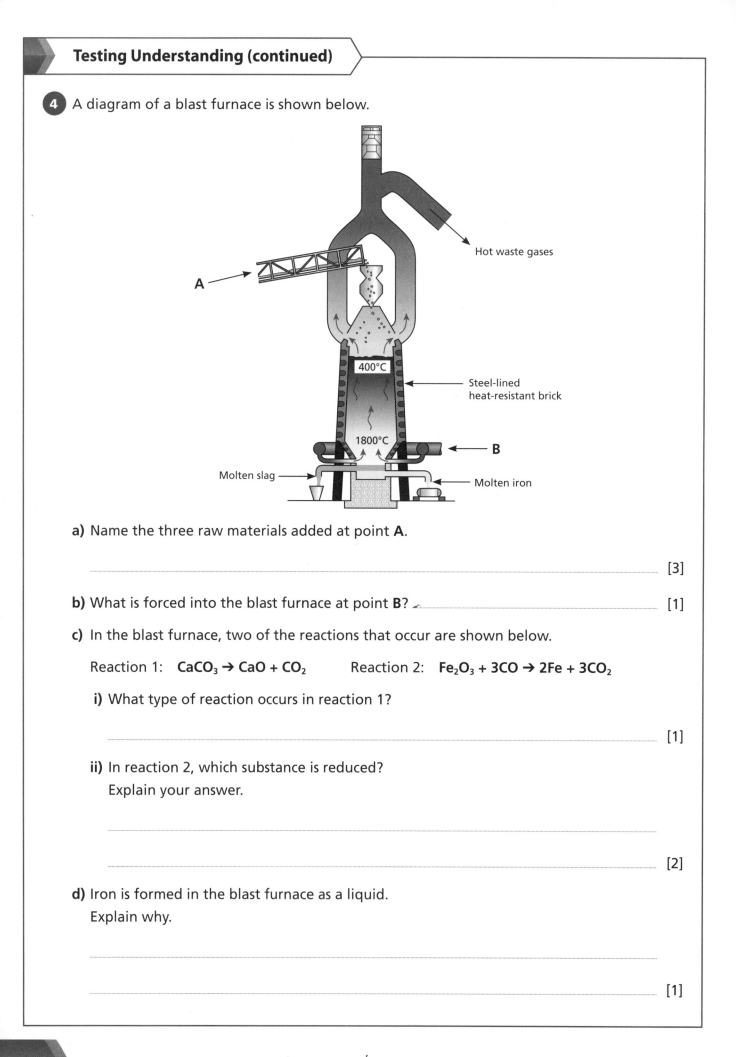

a) Name the three raw materials added at point **A**.

.... [3]

b) What is forced into the blast furnace at point **B**? .... [1]

c) In the blast furnace, two of the reactions that occur are shown below.

Reaction 1: $CaCO_3 \rightarrow CaO + CO_2$ Reaction 2: $Fe_2O_3 + 3CO \rightarrow 2Fe + 3CO_2$

i) What type of reaction occurs in reaction 1?

.... [1]

ii) In reaction 2, which substance is reduced?
Explain your answer.

....

.... [2]

d) Iron is formed in the blast furnace as a liquid.
Explain why.

....

.... [1]

5 The thermite reaction is very exothermic. It is often used to produce liquid iron, which is used to fill gaps in rail tracks. The equation for the thermite reaction is shown below.

$$2Al + Fe_2O_3 \rightarrow Al_2O_3 + 2Fe$$

a) What is meant by the term **exothermic reaction**?

.... [1]

b) In the thermite reaction, which chemical has been oxidised?
Explain your answer.

....

.... [2]

c) By considering the thermite reaction, what can you conclude about the relative positions of aluminium and iron in the reactivity series?
Explain your answer.

....

....

.... [2]

d) Will iron react with aluminium oxide?
Explain your answer.

....

....

.... [2]

6 When the two solids barium hydroxide and ammonium hydroxide are mixed, an endothermic reaction takes place.

a) What is meant by the term **endothermic reaction**?

.... [1]

b) Describe an experiment that you can do to demonstrate that this reaction is endothermic.

....

....

....

.... [3]

Total Marks .... / 45

1 Many chemical reactions can be done in the home.

Becky was investigating whether the reaction between vinegar and baking soda was exothermic or endothermic. She placed some vinegar in a glass and, using a thermometer, recorded the temperature. She noted the reading as 19°C. She then added a spoonful of baking soda and stirred the mixture. She recorded the temperature again and recorded it as 15°C. During the reaction, there was lots of fizzing and bubbling.

a) Was Becky's experiment **exothermic** or **endothermic**?
   Explain your answer.

   ....

   .... [2]

b) The gas produced during this experiment turns limewater milky.
   What is the name of this gas?

   .... [1]

c) Another reaction that can be done in the home is to add indigestion tablets to vinegar.
   This reaction is exothermic.

   i) Without using a thermometer, how can you show that this reaction is exothermic?

      ....

      ....

      .... [2]

   ii) Is energy **absorbed from** or **released to** the surroundings during an
       exothermic reaction?

       .... [1]

2 When a metal reacts with an acid, the metal displaces hydrogen from the acid and heat is given out. The more reactive the metal, the more heat is given out.

Simone was investigating four unknown metals: W, X, Y and Z. She recorded the initial temperature of 25cm³ of acid and then added a spatula of metal powder W. She stirred the mixture and recorded the highest temperature reached by the acid. Simone then repeated the experiment for metals X, Y and Z. Her results are shown in the table at the top of page 37.

Answers

Variation for Survival

Pages 4–15

Vocabulary Builder
1. a) chromosome [1]
   b) gametes [1]
   c) chromosome [1]
   d) gene [1]
   e) species [1]
   f) variation [1]
   g) mutation [1]
   h) clone [1]
2. gametes [1]; fertilisation [1]; genetic information [1]; inherit [1]
3. Extinct [1]
4. nucleus [1]; 46 [1]; DNA [1]; Genes [1]; daughter [1]; parent [1]
5. A single crop grown in an area [1]

Maths Skills
1. a) Discontinuous variation [1]
   b) Group O [1]

   c) There are only four blood groups so the total must be 100%.

   Bar drawn correctly at 4% [1]

Testing Understanding
1. Continuous: height, size of feet, weight
   Discontinuous: eye colour, ear lobe shape, right- or left-handed, ability to roll tongue
   [7 marks: 1 for each characteristic correctly categorised]
2. Don't give one word answers such as 'soil' or 'water' – always clarify what you mean.

   Accept any three from: Availability of water; Minerals; Type of soil; pH of soil; Temperature; Sun / shade (light) [3]
3. **Accept any three from:** When they ripen; Size of fruit; Colour of fruit; Taste of fruit [3]
4. Height is affected by genes, e.g. tall parents are more likely to produce tall offspring. [1]
   Height is affected by environment, e.g. if diet is poor, growth may be stunted. [1]
5. a) There is competition between the individuals for resources [1]. Those that are best adapted are more likely to survive [1] and reproduce [1] and pass on genes to offspring [1].
   b) Darwin [1]; Wallace [1]
6. a) Normal Leopard [1]
   b) Albino Leopard [1]
   c) Normal Leopard [1]
   d) 3 Normal Leopard to 1 Albino Leopard [1]
7. a) Male body cell: 46 chromosomes [1]
   Sperm cell: 23 chromosomes [1]
   Female body cell: 46 chromosomes [1]
   Egg cell: 23 chromosomes [1]
   Embryo: 46 chromosomes [1]
   b) Genes are on chromosomes [1]. Offspring receive half their genes from one parent [1] and half from the other [1].
8. The giraffe's genes are present at birth [1] so cannot change during the giraffe's lifetime [1] or A longer neck acquired through stretching would not affect genes [1] so would not be passed onto offspring [1]
9. An egg / zygote divides in two [1] after fertilisation [1]
10. A: How large the leaves grow [1]
    C: How tall the plant grows [1]
    F: The size of the fruit [1]
11. A: Requires only one parent [1]
    E: Offspring are identical to parent [1]

12. a) Discontinuous variation [1]
    b) If the dominant allele is present, it will 'overpower' any other alleles [1] and the characteristic will show / be evident [1]

    c) It is not a good idea to choose letters where the capital and lower case letter look the same.
    It is always a good idea to add a key if you are not using an obvious letter.

    Parent 1 smooth Tt

	T	t	
T	TT smooth	tT smooth	Key:
t	Tt smooth	tt wrinkled	T = smooth
			t = wrinkled

    (Parent 2 smooth Tt)

    Yes [2 marks: 1 for punnet square; 1 for stating tt = wrinkled (different letters may be used)]
    d) **Accept any two from:** Genes had not yet been discovered; His work was not widely distributed; His results were not easily reproducible [2]

13. Natural disasters, such as a meteor strike, will lead to climate change.

    Accept any two from: Climate change (or named climate change); Supervolcano eruption; Fall in sea level; Introduction of predators / non-native species; Hunting [2]
14. Choosing characteristics that are desired [1]. Selecting parents with those characteristics [1] and breeding them to produce offspring with the desired characteristics [1].
15. a) T [1]
    b) F [1]
    c) F [1]
    d) T [1]
    e) T [1]
    f) T [1]
16. 2, 4, 1, 5, 3 [2 marks for all correct; 1 mark if any two are in the wrong order]
17. **Accept any two from:** Diagnosis of medical conditions / disease; Genetic engineering; Forensic science; Gene banks; Family tree / history [2]
18. a) DNA [1]
    b) Nucleus [1]
    c) **Accept any two from:** Watson; Crick; Wilkins; Franklin [2]
    d) Mutation [1]
    e) 4 [1]
19. **Accept any two from:** Sheep can be farmed on areas that are not presently used for farming; It allows fields to be used for other livestock / growing crops; Seaweed is abundant / easily available [2]
20. a) i) pollen [1]
       ii) stigma [1]
       iii) seeds [1]
       iv) Plant [1]
    b) Selective breeding [1]
21. A: It allows us to group organisms by observing typical features [1]
    D: It helps us to clarify the relationship between organisms [1]
22. **Accept any two from:** Bulbs; Corms; Tubers; Runners; Rhizomes [2]

Working Scientifically
1. a) A mutation occurred [1]
   b) They would be camouflaged from predators [1]

c) **Accept either:** The sample area in the forest; The type of forest [1]

d) **Accept either:** The weather; The number / type of predators in the forest [1]

e)
> Only use the information in the text to answer the question.

A: More dark moths than pale moths survived in the Birmingham forest. [1]

D: Pale moths do not survive as well as dark moths in forests exposed to pollution. [1]

Science in Use

1. a) A species at risk of extinction [1]
   b) Deforestation [1]; Pollution [1]
   c) Captive breeding uses live animals [1], whereas gene banks store DNA [1]
   d) **Accept either:** Less space is needed for gene banks; Captive breeding programmes are not always successful [1]
   e) Increased variation means more chance of a breed surviving [1] if affected by adverse conditions **(accept a named example from disease, food shortage, natural disaster)** [1]

2. a) Mouflon sheep, because $\frac{1}{7}$ (or 14%) of the embryos resulted in a successful live birth [1] compared to only $\frac{5}{401}$ (or 1.2%) for the pig [1]
   b) For: **Accept either:** It would save human lives; It would create a supply of organs for use in transplants [1]
   Against: Some people believe it is unethical because animals have a right to live / animals are killed [1]
   c) **Accept either:** There will be no genetic variation; It will result in a smaller gene pool [1]

Our Health and the Effects of Drugs

Pages 16–27

Vocabulary Builder

1. a) recreational [1]
   b) nicotine [1]
   c) anaemia [1]
   d) stimulant [1]
   e) carcinogen [1]
   f) antibiotic [1]
   g) toxin [1]
2. single-celled [1]; nucleus [1]; cytoplasm [1]; pathogens [1]; antibiotics [1]; resistance [1]; mutate [1]
3. a) oxygen [1]
   b) antibodies [1]
   c) clot [1]
   d) antivirals [1]
   e) bone marrow [1]
   f) liver [1]
4. a) cholera [1]; because the others are all caused by viruses [1]
   b) cocaine [1]; because the others are all legal drugs [1]
   c) lymphocyte [1]; because the others are all microbes [1]
5. When the body becomes physically [1] dependent [1] on a drug.
6. a) side effect [1]
   b) cilia [1]
   c) class A [1]
   d) infectious [1]
   e) Viruses [1]
7. First line – form a barrier [1] to stop microbes entering the body [1]
   Second line – involves white blood cells [1], which attack microbes [1] after they have entered the body [1]
8. weakened [1]; immune response [1]; White [1]; antibodies [1]; memory cells [1]

Maths Skills

1. a)
> Always clarify rise or fall in numbers with supporting figures.

The number of bacteria stayed the same [1] for the first ten hours [1], and then rose rapidly [1] during the next ten hours [1] to 10 million. The number then stayed the same for 15 hours [1] before falling [1].

b) **Accept either:** The bacteria ran out of resources / food / nutrients; The bacteria were killed by accumulation / the effect of toxic waste products [1]

c) C: The number of live bacteria will start to increase at 20 hours. [1]

2. a)
> When making a comparison, remember to use comparative words, e.g. 'faster' rather than 'fast'.

When exposed to the pathogen following vaccination, the response is faster [1] and higher levels of antibodies are produced [1]

b)
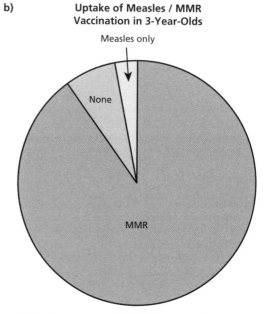
Uptake of Measles / MMR Vaccination in 3-Year-Olds

Measles only

None

MMR

[All sectors correct with labels = 2 marks; 1 sector correct with labels = 1 mark; all sectors correct but no labels = 1 mark]

Testing Understanding

1. a) Liver [1]
   b) Placenta [1]
   c) memory loss [1]; decreased coordination [1]
2. Down's syndrome – Genetically inherited
   Cholera – Bacteria
   Chickenpox – Virus
   Scurvy – Vitamin C deficiency
   [All correct = 3 marks; 2 correct = 2 marks; 1 correct = 1 mark]
3. a) **Accept any one from:** Multiple sclerosis; AIDS; Cancer [1]
   b) **Accept any two from:** Cancer; Brain damage; Decreased fertility; Mental health problems [2]
4. a) Nicotine [1]
   b) Tar [1]
   c) Tar [1]
   d) Carbon monoxide [1]
   e) Carbon monoxide [1]
5. a) Legal: aspirin, antibiotics, caffeine
   Illegal: cannabis, speed, ecstasy
   [6 marks: 1 for each drug correctly categorised]
   b) Withdrawal [1]
6. They produce antibodies [1]; They produce antitoxins [1]; They engulf microbes (phagocytosis) [1]
7. a) F [1]
   b) T [1]
   c) T [1]
   d) F [1]
   e) F [1]
   f) F [1]

8. a) Platelet [1]
   b) Because it stops bacteria entering the body [1]
9. 7, 2, 4, 1, 5, 8, 3, 6
   [3 marks: 1 for steps 2 and 3 in the correct order; 1 for steps 4 and 5 in the correct order; 1 for steps 6 and 7 (in either order) as the last two steps before step 8]
10. a) Kills microbes [1]
    b) Mucus traps microbes [1]; Cilia move it upwards away from the lungs [1]
    c) Acts as a physical barrier (accept: produces sweat, which has antibacterial properties) [1]
    d) Contain antimicrobial substances [1]
11. warmth [1]; moisture [1]; food [1]
12. Bacteria: tuberculosis, salmonella food poisoning, cholera
    Fungus: athlete's foot
    Virus: chickenpox, mumps, influenza, measles
    [8 marks: 1 for each disease correctly categorised]
13. Alcohol – Depressant
    LSD – Hallucinogen
    Morphine – Painkiller
    Caffeine – Stimulant
    [All correct = 3 marks; 2 correct = 2 marks; 1 correct = 1 mark]
14. Emotional: anxiety, insomnia, depression
    Physical: vomiting, diarrhoea, shaking
    [6 marks: 1 for each symptom correctly categorised]
15. During exercise, more oxygen [1] is needed to provide energy [1], but carbon monoxide [1] in cigarette smoke binds with haemoglobin [1] in red blood cells [1] in place of oxygen [1]
16. a) Malaria – Animals
    HIV – Blood / bodily fluids
    Cholera – Water / food
    Colds – Air
    [All correct = 3 marks; 2 correct = 2 marks; 1 correct = 1 mark]
    b) By encouraging use of antiseptic [1] hand wash [1] when moving between patients / wards [1]
17. a) A strain of bacteria that is resistant [1] to many different antibiotics [1]
    b) A few bacteria are resistant [1] to the antibiotic that is prescribed [1]. The antibiotic kills the sensitive (non-resistant) bacteria [1], allowing the resistant bacteria to multiply to produce a large population [1].
    c) Accept either: Rod; Spiral [1]

Working Scientifically
1. a) inoculating loop [1]
   b) To kill any bacteria / sterilise it [1]
   c) Accept either: For health and safety reasons / To stop any microbes that grow from getting out of the Petri dish [1]
   d) 25°C [1]
   e) 1–2 days [1]
2. a) Accept any one from: They didn't measure the heart rate of each person at the start of the experiment; They didn't measure the rise in heart rate; The same person was not used for water and coffee [1]
   b) Whether they have drunk coffee or not [1]
   c) Heart rate [1]
   d) By taking his pulse [1]
   e) Expect it to increase [1]
3. a) Slide [1]
   b) The stage [1]
   c) A white blood cell / phagocyte [1]

Science in Use
1. a) By air [1]; Through contact with a contaminated surface / material [1]
   b) Flu is caused by a virus [1]; Antibiotics are not effective against viruses [1]
   c) Accept any one from: Children; The elderly; People with existing respiratory problems; People who are immunologically compromised [1]
   d) The flu virus changes regularly [1], so antibodies may not recognise the new strain [1]

Obtaining Useful Materials

Pages 28–39

Vocabulary Builder
1. B: Ores [1]
2. Ceramics – Formed by the heating and subsequent cooling of an inorganic material, e.g. clay
   Polymers – Formed by joining together lots of small molecules
   Composites – Formed by combining two different materials that often have very different properties
   [All correct = 2 marks; 1 correct = 1 mark]
3. C: Thermal decomposition [1]
4. C: Displacement [1]
5. a) reduction [1]
   b) endothermic [1]
   c) Remember 'exit' refers to the way out, so **exothermic** refers to heat being given out.

   exothermic [1]

Maths Skills
1. a) Oreland: £150 [1]
   Mineralstan: £190 [1]
   b) Oreland [1], because the profit is £200 – (£100 + £50) = £50 [1]. In Mineralstan, the profit is £200 – (£120 + £70) = £10 [1].
   c) The new mining cost is £75 [1], so the total cost of production will be £175 [1]. Profit = £200 – £175 = £25 [1].
   d) No, Oreland will not still produce aluminium [1], because the total cost of extraction will be £250, which is higher than the selling price [1]
2. a) Always show your working when doing calculations.

   23.65g – 20.45g [1] = 3.2g [1]
   b) 23.01g – 20.45g [1] = 2.56g [1]
   c) 3.2g – 2.56g [1] = 0.64g [1]
   d) Try to picture yourself doing the experiment when answering questions about practical work. This will help you to visualise what happened during the experiment.

   $\frac{2.56}{3.2} \times 100$ [1] = 80% [1]

Testing Understanding
1. a) The metals in order of reactivity [1]
   b) They are reactive and so combine with other elements [1]
   c) Accept any one from: Potassium; Sodium; Calcium [1]
   d) Above copper, because X displaces copper from copper oxide [1]; Below iron, because X is unable to displace iron from iron oxide [1]; Therefore, X should be placed between iron and copper [1]
   e) A higher temperature [1]; The more reactive the metal the higher the temperature at which the metal carbonate decomposes [1]
2. a) Because they are not very reactive / they are low in the reactivity series [1]
   b) A rock that contains enough quantities of a metal [1] to make it worthwhile extracting the metal from it [1]
   c) Mining [1]
   d) PbO / lead oxide [1]; It has lost oxygen [1]
   e) The reactivity series is very useful for helping to explain why displacement reactions do or do not occur.

   A more reactive element (in this case, carbon) [1] takes the place of a less reactive element (in this case, lead) in a compound [1]
   f) Copper is less reactive [1] than lead, so a displacement reaction would not occur [1]
   g) Magnesium is much more expensive than carbon (accept: magnesium has to be extracted and is therefore costly) [1], so it is not economically viable to use magnesium instead of carbon to extract lead [1]

h)

Lead	Carbon Dioxide
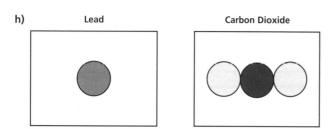	

[2 marks: 1 for each correct diagram]

3. a) T [1]
   b) T [1]
   c) F [1]
   d) T [1]
4. a) **In any order:** Iron ore / haematite [1]; Coke [1]; Limestone [1]
   b) (Hot) air [1]
   c) i) Thermal decomposition (**accept:** endothermic) [1]
      ii) Fe_2O_3 / iron oxide [1], as this substance loses oxygen [1]
   d) The temperature in the blast furnace is above the melting point of iron [1]
5. a) A reaction that produces heat [1]
   b) Al / Aluminium [1], as it has gained oxygen [1]
   c) Aluminium must be higher than iron [1] because aluminium is able to displace iron from iron oxide [1]
   d) No [1]; Iron is below aluminium in the reactivity series, so it is not able to displace aluminium from aluminium oxide [1]
6. a) A reaction that absorbs heat from the surroundings [1]
   b) Insert a thermometer into one of the solids and record the temperature [1]; Add the other solid and stir (e.g. with the thermometer), then record the final temperature [1]; The final temperature is lower than the initial temperature in an endothermic reaction [1]

Working Scientifically

1. a) Endothermic [1], because the temperature decreased [1]
   b) Carbon dioxide [1]
   c) i) Place your hands around a cup containing the vinegar with the indigestion tablets added [1]; Your hands will get warmer, proving that the reaction is exothermic [1]
      ii) Released to the surroundings [1]
2. a) W: 6
      X: 0
      Y: 14
      Z: 11
      [1 mark for all four correct]
   b) Salt [1] + Hydrogen [1]
   c)
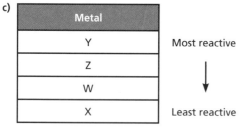

Metal	
Y	Most reactive
Z	
W	
X	Least reactive

[2 marks for all four in the correct order; 1 mark for two in the correct order]
   d) Metal X [1]; There was no temperature change when this metal was added to the acid, meaning that there was no reaction. As there was no reaction, metal X must be below hydrogen in the reactivity series. [1]

Science in Use

1. a) **Accept any two from:** High melting point; Strong; Lightweight; Easily moulded into shape; Chemically unreactive [2]

b) By the heating and subsequent cooling [1] of an inorganic (not carbon-containing) liquid [1]
   c) A polymer [1]
   d) **Accept any two from:** Light; Easily moulded into shape; Able to withstand strong forces; Strong [2]
2. a) Carbon dioxide [1]
   b) Global warming (contributing to the greenhouse effect) [1]
   c) Certain gases, such as carbon dioxide, trap energy from the Sun in the atmosphere [1], which causes a warming effect [1]

Using Our Earth Sustainably

Pages 40–49

Vocabulary Builder

1. a) photosynthesis [1]
   b) decay [1]
   c) respiration [1]
   d) combustion [1]
2. B: Wood [1]
3. Igneous – Formed by the cooling and solidifying of liquid magma or lava
   Metamorphic – Formed by the effects of heat and pressure on other types of rock
   Sedimentary – Formed by compacting and cementing lots of small pieces of rock
   [All correct = 2 marks; 1 correct = 1 mark]
4. a) F [1]
   b) T [1]
   c) T [1]
   d) T [1]
   e) F [1]
5. D: Deposition [1]

Maths Skills

1. 21% [1]
2. a) 0.028% [1]
   b)

> When estimating from a graph, use a ruler and draw lines from the axes to the curve to help you. A degree of tolerance above and below the correct answer will be allowed.

   Any answer between 1963 and 1974 [1]
   c) C: 1900–1950 [1]
   d) Any answer between 0.037 and 0.040, given to 2 s.f. [1]

Testing Understanding

1. B: Sedimentary [1]
2. A: Photosynthesis [1]
3. a) T [1]
   b) T [1]
   c) F [1]
   d) T [1]
4. A: Crust
   B: Mantle
   C: Outer core
   D: Inner core
   [All correct = 3 marks; 2 correct = 2 marks; 1 correct = 1 mark]
5. **Accept any two from:** To preserve (the Earth's) natural resources; To reduce pollution; To reduce the energy costs of disposing of waste [2]
6. a) A: Photosynthesis
      B: Respiration
      C: Combustion
      D: Decay
      E: Fossil fuels
      [All correct = 4 marks; 3 correct = 3 marks, 2 correct = 2 marks; 1 correct = 1 mark]

b) The amount of carbon dioxide would increase [1] as less would be removed from the atmosphere by photosynthesis [1]

c) The amount of carbon dioxide would decrease [1] as burning fossil fuels releases carbon dioxide into the atmosphere [1]

7. **a)** A: Igneous
   B: Metamorphic
   C: Sedimentary
   [All correct = 2 marks; 1 correct = 1 mark]
   b) i) The natural breakdown of rocks [1]
      ii) Accept any one from: Freeze-thaw; Root growth; Exfoliation / onion skin weathering (i.e. the constant heating and cooling of rocks causing rocks to break apart); Acid rain; Mechanical weathering (e.g. wave action) [1]
   c) Accept either: From volcanoes; At the join of tectonic plates [1]

8. **a)** A: Igneous [1]
   b) As lava / magma cools and solidifies [1], crystals of minerals in the lava / magma form [1]
   c) Rock B [1], because it has smaller crystals [1]

Working Scientifically

1. **a)** The salol [1]; It is a liquid that forms crystals when it cools [1]
   b) By using either hot or cold microscope slides [1]
   c) Temperature [1]
   d) Crystal size [1]
   e) **Crystals Formed on Cold Slides**

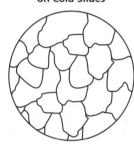

   [1 mark for showing smaller crystals than on the warm slides]

   f)
   > Remember that the longer it takes for the magma / lava to cool, the more time crystals have to grow.

   Intrusive [1]; The lava cools and solidifies inside the Earth's crust, which means that it solidifies more slowly, forming larger crystals [1]

Science in Use

1. **a)** The rainforests absorb lots of carbon dioxide and release lots of oxygen [1]; This is similar to the process of gas exchange that occurs in the lungs (note that the lungs take in oxygen from the air and release carbon dioxide) [1]
   b) It increases carbon dioxide levels [1]; Trees remove carbon dioxide from the atmosphere by photosynthesis, and fewer trees means less photosynthesis [1]
   c) Increased carbon dioxide levels are thought to contribute to global warming [1], which could lead to further environmental problems, e.g. melting of the polar ice caps [1]

   d)
   > When the term **suggest** is used in a question, it means that you can apply your own thoughts and ideas.

   Carbon dioxide is a gas and so it is expensive to collect [1], it is also expensive to separate carbon dioxide from other gases [1] and it is expensive to transport / store carbon dioxide gas underground [1]

2. **a)** Burning fossil fuels [1]; Cutting down rainforests [1]
   b) Accept any two from: Photosynthesis; Dissolving in oceans; Forming shells / rocks [2]
   c) Global warming [1]

Motion on Earth and in Space

Pages 50–60

Vocabulary Builder

1. gravity [1]; weight [1]; downwards [1]
2. star [1]; fusion [1]; hydrogen [1]; helium [1]; red giant [1]
3. C, B, E, D, A [1]
4. orbit [1]; ellipse [1]; year [1]; gravitational [1]
5. A light year is the distance travelled (or covered) [1] by light in one year [1]
6. Mass is the amount of matter an object contains [1]; Units of mass are kg [1]
   Weight is a force [1] that depends on the strength of the gravitational field [1]; Units of weight are newtons [1]

Maths Skills

1. **a)** Weight = Mass × Gravitational field strength on Earth [1]
      Weight = 72 × 10 = 720N [1]
   b) Weight = Mass × Gravitational field strength on Mars [1]
      Weight = 72 × 3.7 = 266.4N **(accept: 270N)** [1]

2.
   > Change speed from metres per second to kilometres per second.

   Speed = $\frac{Distance}{Time}$, so Time = $\frac{Distance}{Speed}$

   Time = 150 000 000km ÷ 300 000km/s = 500 seconds [1]
   500 ÷ 60 = 8.33 … [1] = 8 minutes [1]

3. **a)** 3.7 years [1]
   b)
   > Change time (3.7 years) into seconds and speed (300 000 000m/s) into km/s.

   Distance = Speed × Time [1]
   = 300 000 × 3.7 × 31 600 000 [1]
   Distance = 35 000 000 000 000km or 3.5×10^{13}km (to 2 s.f.) **(accept answer in standard form)** [1]

4.

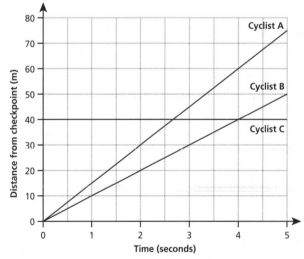

   [6 marks: 1 for each line correctly plotted; 1 for each line correctly labelled]

5. **a)** 112 – 96 = 16km/h [1]
   b) 96 – 112 = –16km/h **(accept: 16km/h in the opposite direction)** **[2 marks: 1 for 16km/h; 1 for giving the direction ('–' or 'opposite direction')]**
   c) 96 – (–112) [1] = 208km/h [1] **(accept: 112 – (–96) = 208km/h)**

Testing Understanding
1. a) T [1]
   b) T [1]
   c) F [1]
   d) T [1]
   e) F [1]
2. a) Latitude means an angular position on the Earth's surface [1], measured from the equator [1]
   b) 12 hours [1]
   c) i) 12 hours [1]
      ii) 24 hours [1]

3.

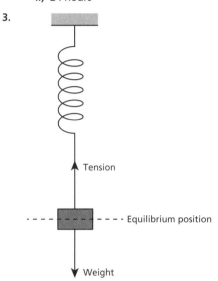

[4 marks: 1 for showing the equilibrium position; 1 for showing weight acting downwards; 1 for showing tension (in spring) acting upwards; 1 for showing the forces as arrows of approximately equal length from the equilibrium position]

4.

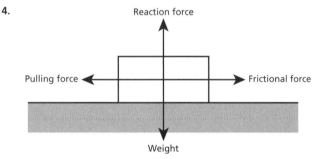

[4 marks: 1 for representing all four forces as arrows; 1 for drawing the reaction and weight arrows the same length; 1 for drawing the pull and friction arrows the same length; 1 for drawing the reaction and weight forces vertically]

5. a) Weight, Air resistance [1]
   b) Weight, Tension (in spring) [1]
   c) Weight, Reaction force [1]
   d) i)–ii) In either order:
      Weight, Upthrust [1]
      Driving force, Air resistance [1]

Working Scientifically
1. a) Load values: 1, 2, 3, 4, 5, 6, 7, 8, 9, 10
      [2 marks for all correct; 1 mark for nine correct]

b) i)

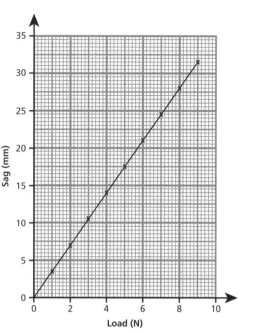

[2 marks for all points correctly plotted based on values from part a); 1 mark for eight points correctly plotted]

   ii) Best straight line drawn between the points (a ruler must be used) [1]
      Gradient = 31.5 ÷ 9 [1] = 3.5mm/N (to 2 s.f.) [1] or
      Gradient = 0.0315 ÷ 9 [1] = 0.0035m/N (to 2 s.f.) [1]
c) Sag is (directly) proportional to the load (accept: it obeys Hooke's Law) [1]
d) The ruler broke [1]
e) i) 4.6 ± 0.2N (accept correct value read from student's graph) [1]
   ii) 29.5 ± 0.5mm (accept correct value read from student's graph) [1]
f) i) From the supports (accept: pivot points) [1]
   ii) The upward force increases [1]
g) i) Two rulers would be stiffer (accept similar explanation) [1]
   ii) Less sag would be produced [1]
h) Repeat the experiment [1]

Science in Use
1. a) Mass (accept: density) [1]; Radius (accept: size) [1]
   b) i) The gravitational field strength increases [1]
      ii) The gravitational field strength decreases [1]
   c) i) $\frac{Mass}{Radius^2} \times 1\,000\,000 = \frac{17\,200}{22\,300^2} \times 1\,000\,000$ [1]
      $= 34.58\ldots$ [1] = 35 (to 2 s.f.) [1]
      ii) From the graph:
         Gravitational field strength = 14 ± 1N/kg (accept correct value read from graph based on student's answer to part i)) [1]
   d) i) From the graph: Mass–radius index = 12 ± 1 [1]
      ii)
      $\frac{Mass}{Radius^2} \times 1\,000\,000 = 12$, so you can rearrange this as $Radius^2 = \frac{Mass \times 1\,000\,000}{12}$.

      $Radius^2 = \frac{15 \times 1\,000\,000}{12}$ [1] = 1\,250\,000 [1]

      $Radius = \sqrt{1\,250\,000} = 1118.03\ldots$ [1] = 1100km (to 2 s.f.) [1]
   e) i) $\frac{Mass}{Radius^2} \times 1\,000\,000 = \frac{333\,000\,000}{696\,000^2} \times 1\,000\,000$ [1]
      $= 687.4\ldots$ [1] = 687 (to 3 s.f.) [1]
      ii) From the graph: a mass–radius index value of 68.7 (≈69) corresponds to a gravitational field strength of 27 ± 1N/kg [1]
         Therefore, 687 (68.7 × 10) corresponds to 270 ± 10N/kg (27 × 10) (accept answer deduced from correct value read from graph based on student's answer to part i)) [1]

Waves and Energy Transfer

Pages 61–70

Vocabulary Builder

1. If their wave crests coincide **[1]**, two waves add together to make a bigger wave **[1]**; If the crest of one wave coincides with the trough of another wave **[1]**, the two waves cancel each other and no wave is produced **[1] (accept similar explanation)**

2.

Sound Waves	Light Waves
mechanical	electromagnetic
longitudinal	transverse
330m/s	300 000 000m/s
needs a medium	can travel through a vacuum

   [4 marks: 1 for each pair of properties correctly categorised]

3. Casts no shadow – Transparent
   Casts a weak shadow – Translucent
   Casts a strong shadow – Opaque
   [All correct = 2 marks; 1 correct = 1 mark]

4. Heat is energy **(accept: energy transfer) [1]**; Temperature is a measure of energy **[1]**

5. Diffuse scattering: Reflection from a rough surface **[1]**; Light reflected in many different directions **[1]**
   Specular reflection: Reflection from a flat, smooth surface **[1]**; Light reflected in the same direction **[1]**

6. a) F **[1]**
   b) T **[1]**
   c) T **[1]**

7. Energy cannot be created or destroyed **[1]**, it can only be transformed from one form into another **[1]**

8. a) Pollutants in the atmosphere **[1]** react **[1]** in the presence of sunlight **[1]**
   b) Nitrogen dioxide **[1]** + Sunlight **[1]** → Nitrogen monoxide **[1]** + Oxygen **[1]**

9. a) **Accept either:** (thermal) conduction; convection **[1]**
   b) rainbow **[1]**
   c) refraction **[1]**
   d) wavelength **[1]**
   e) convex **[1]**

Maths Skills

1. Change in temperature = 50 – 20 = 30°C **[1]**
   Energy transferred (J) = Mass (kg) × 4200 × Change in temp (°C), so Energy = 0.3 × 4200 × 30 **[1]** = 37 800J **[1]** = 38kJ (to 2 s.f.) **[1]**

2. a) 2.15kW = 2150W **[1]** = 2150J/s **[1]**
   b) 6 350 000J = 6.35MJ **[1]**
   c) 8 460 000J = 8460kJ **[1]**

   $\frac{8460}{3600}$ **[1]** = 2.35kWh **[1]**

3.
   > There are 60 × 60 = 3600 seconds in 1 hour.

   40W = 40J/s **[1]**
   Energy transfer (J) = Power (W) × Time (seconds)
   = 40 × 8 × 3600 **[1]** = 1 152 000J **[1]** = 1.152MJ = 1.2MJ (to 2 s.f.) **[1]**

4. Change in temperature = 100 – 20 = 80°C **[1]**
   Energy transfer = 0.35 × 4200 × 80 **[1]** = 117 600J **[1]** = 117.6kJ = 120kJ (to 2 s.f.) **[1]**

5. Gas: 650 × 0.04 **[1]** = £26.00 **[1]**
   Electricity: 400 × 0.13 **[1]** = £52.00 **[1]**
   Total cost = 26 + 52 = £78.00 **[1]**

6.
   > 1kJ = 0.240kcal, so you need to multiply by 0.240 to convert from kilojoules to kilocalories.

   779kJ = 779 × 0.240 **[1]** = 186.96kcal **[1]** = 187kcal (to the nearest kilocalorie) **[1]**

Testing Understanding

1. Insulator: A material that does not transfer energy well **[1]**
   Conductor: A material that transfers energy well **[1]**

2.

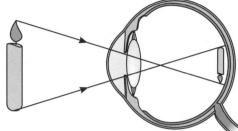

   [4 marks: 1 for drawing two additional light rays from the object (candle) passing through the lens; 1 for including arrows on both light rays; 1 for showing both light rays crossing over before reaching the retina; 1 for showing the image (of the candle) inverted]

3. Light rays from the Sun **[1]** are reflected from the Moon's surface **[1]**

4. a)

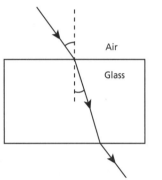

   [3 marks: 1 for drawing the light ray inside the glass block and refracted as it leaves the glass block; 1 for including arrows on the light ray; 1 for drawing the light ray leaving the glass block parallel to the light ray entering the glass block]
   b) The light ray inside the block has a shorter wavelength **(accept: slower speed) [1]**. The light ray leaving the block has the same wavelength as the light ray entering the block **[1]**.

5. 4 **[1]** cycles per second **or** Hertz **(accept: Hz) [1]**

6. **Accept any three from:** Thermal; Chemical; Gravitational; Kinetic; Elastic; Magnetic **[3]**

7. As the metal is heated, energy is transferred to the particles **[1]**. The particles vibrate faster **[1]**. They transfer energy as they continually collide with their neighbours **[1]**. Energy is transferred through the entire length of the rod **[1]**. The opposite end becomes hot **[1]**.

Working Scientifically

1. a) With lid: The coffee cools **[1]**; The rate of cooling is gradual / fairly constant **[1]**
   Without lid: The coffee cools **[1]**; The rate of cooling is fast initially **[1]**, but gradually decreases **[1]**
   b) **Accept either:** Room temperature; 20°C **[1]**
   c) With lid: 10 ± 0.5 minutes **[1]**
   Without lid: 3.7 ± 0.5 minutes **[1]**
   d) With lid: Temperature difference between 3 and 5 minutes = 6°C **[1]**; Rate of cooling = $\frac{6}{2}$ = 3°C/min **(accept: 3 ± 1°C/min) [1]**
   Without lid: Temperature difference between 3 and 5 minutes = 9°C **[1]**; Rate of cooling = $\frac{9}{2}$ = 4.5°C/min **(accept: 4.5 ± 1°C/min) [1]**

e) Heat is lost through thermal conduction **[1]** between the cup and the surface it is resting on **[1]**, from radiation **[1]** into the surrounding air **[1]** and through convection **[1]**

f) A paper cup with a lid retains the heat longer **[1]** than one without a lid **[1]**

Science in Use

1. a)

Remember that 1W = 1J/s.

80W = 80J/s
8 hours = 8 × 60 × 60 = 28 800s   **[1]**
Energy required = 80 × 28 800 **[1]** = 2 304 000J **[1]**
           = 2304kJ   **[1]**
Converting this to kcal = 2304 × 0.240 = 552.96kcal
           = 550kcal (to 2 s.f.)   **[1]**

b) Energy used in jogging = 400 × 20 × 60 = 480 000J = 480kJ **[1]**
Converting this to kcal = 480 × 0.240 = 115.2kcal   **[1]**
Energy used in swimming = 500 × 15 × 60 = 450 000J = 450kJ **[1]**
Converting this to kcal = 450 × 0.240 = 108kcal   **[1]**
Total energy expenditure = 115.2 + 108
           = 223.2kcal = 220kcal (to 2 s.f.)   **[1]**

c) i) No, it wouldn't be sufficient **[1]**. The energy available in one bar is 214kcal **[1]**, whereas the energy required for the exercise is 220kcal (to 2 s.f.).

ii) **Accept any one from:** Nyoko's BMR has been ignored; All of the energy in the bar has been used/not used; Nyoko had an energy reserve at the start of the exercise routine **(accept any other suitable assumption)**   **[1]**

d) Jasmine requires a higher energy intake than Nyoko   **[1]**

e) In a 60g bar, there are 214kcal   **[1]**
Therefore, 1g = $\frac{214}{60}$ kcal   **[1]**
There are 23g of sugar in a bar:
23g = 23 × $\frac{214}{60}$ **[1]** = 82.0 ... = 82kcal (to 2 s.f.) **[1]**

f) 3 hours = 3 × 60 × 60 = 10 800s   **[1]**
Energy required = 400 × 10 800 = 4 320 000J = 4320kJ   **[1]**
Converting this to kcal = 4320 × 0.240
           = 1036.8 = 1000kcal (to 2 s.f.)   **[1]**

Metal	Initial Temperature (°C)	Final Temperature (°C)	Temperature Change (°C)
W	18	24	
X	19	19	
Y	20	34	
Z	18	29	

a) Calculate the temperature change for each metal.
Write your answers in the table. [1]

b) Complete the word equation below for the reaction that occurs when a metal reacts with an acid.

Acid + Metal ➔ _metal oxide_ + _____ [2]

c) Complete the table below, placing the metals in order of reactivity.

Metal

Most reactive

↓

Least reactive [2]

d) One of the metals is below hydrogen in the reactivity series. Which one?
Explain your answer.

_____

_____

_____

_____

_____

_____ [2]

Total Marks _____ / 13

1 Read the passage below about materials and then answer the questions that follow.

Scientists are constantly developing materials for new uses. For example, **ceramic tiles** have been used to cover space shuttles to protect them upon re-entry into the Earth's atmosphere. If you look carefully at the photograph below of the shuttle Explorer OV100, you can see some of these tiles.

Some **man-made materials** are produced by joining together lots of small molecules. One such material is **Kevlar®**, which is used in bulletproof jackets as worn by the journalist in the photograph below.

a) State two properties of ceramics that make them suitable for use in space shuttles.

....

.... [2]

b) How are ceramics made?

....

.... [2]

c) What type of man-made material is Kevlar®?

.... [1]

d) Give two properties that you think Kevlar® possesses that make it suitable for use in bulletproof clothing.

....

.... [2]

2 Read the passage below about iron and then answer the questions that follow.

Most of the iron extracted from its ores is used to make steel in factories such as the one pictured.

The processes of mining, extracting metals from ores using carbon, and then using them in the production of other materials such as steel, involves the production of **waste gases** that are frequently released into the atmosphere, as shown in the picture.

a) Name the main carbon-containing gas that is released into the atmosphere during the extraction of metals.

.... [1]

b) State one environmental problem that this gas is thought to cause.

.... [1]

c) Explain what is meant by the term **greenhouse effect**.

....

....

.... [2]

Total Marks .... / 11

	Vocabulary Builder	Maths Skills	Testing Understanding	Working Scientifically	Science in Use
Total Marks	.... / 8	.... / 18	.... / 45	.... / 13	.... / 11

Vocabulary Builder

1. The words in the box are all associated with the carbon cycle.
   Use these words to complete the sentences below.

decay	photosynthesis	respiration	combustion

a) The process of _photosynthesis_ involves green coloured plants making
   energy-containing molecules from carbon dioxide and water using energy from
   the sunlight.   [1]

b) The process of _decay_ occurs when plants and animals die.   [1]

c) When plants and animals release energy from food, _respiration_
   is occurring.   [1]

d) The _combustion_ of fossil fuels releases carbon dioxide back into
   the atmosphere.   [1]

2. Which one of the following is **not** a **fossil fuel**?
   Underline the correct option.

   A: Coal   B: Wood

   C: Natural gas   D: Oil   [1]

3. Draw lines to match each rock type to the correct description of how it is formed.

Type of Rock	Formation

| Igneous |
| Metamorphic |
| Sedimentary |

Formed by compacting and cementing lots of small pieces of rock

Formed by the effects of heat and pressure on other types of rock

Formed by the cooling and solidifying of liquid magma or lava   [2]

4 Which of the following statements about the Earth's structure are true (**T**) and which are false (**F**)?

Write **T** or **F** in the spaces provided.

a) The atmosphere is a layer of the Earth. ....F........ [1]

b) The mantle is a layer of the Earth. ....T........ [1]

c) One of the Earth's layers is called the crust. ....T........ [1]

d) The Earth has a layer known as the outer core. ....T........ [1]

e) The inner core is a liquid. ....T........ [1]

5 Which one of the following is **not** a way in which rocks are broken down naturally in the environment?

Underline the correct option.

   A: Dissolving by acid rain   **B:** Freeze-thaw

   C: Tree roots   **D:** Deposition   [1]

Total Marks .... / 13

Maths Skills

1 The pie chart below shows the composition of gases in the atmosphere today. Calculate the missing percentage (x) for oxygen.

The Composition of Gases in the Atmosphere Today

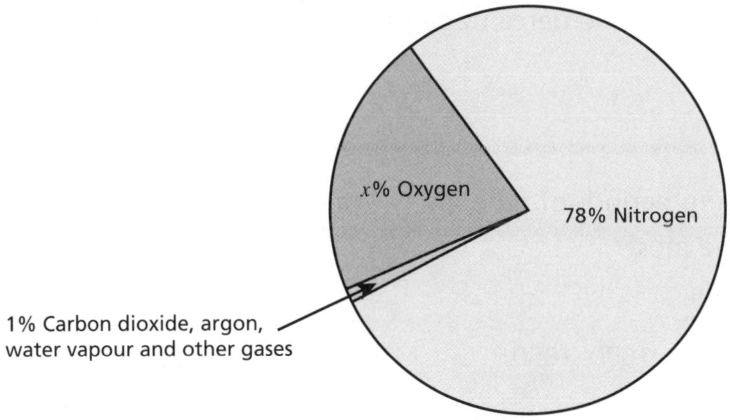

x% Oxygen

78% Nitrogen

1% Carbon dioxide, argon, water vapour and other gases

.... [1]

31%

2 The graph below shows how the amount of carbon dioxide in the atmosphere changed from the year 1700 to the end of the 20th century.

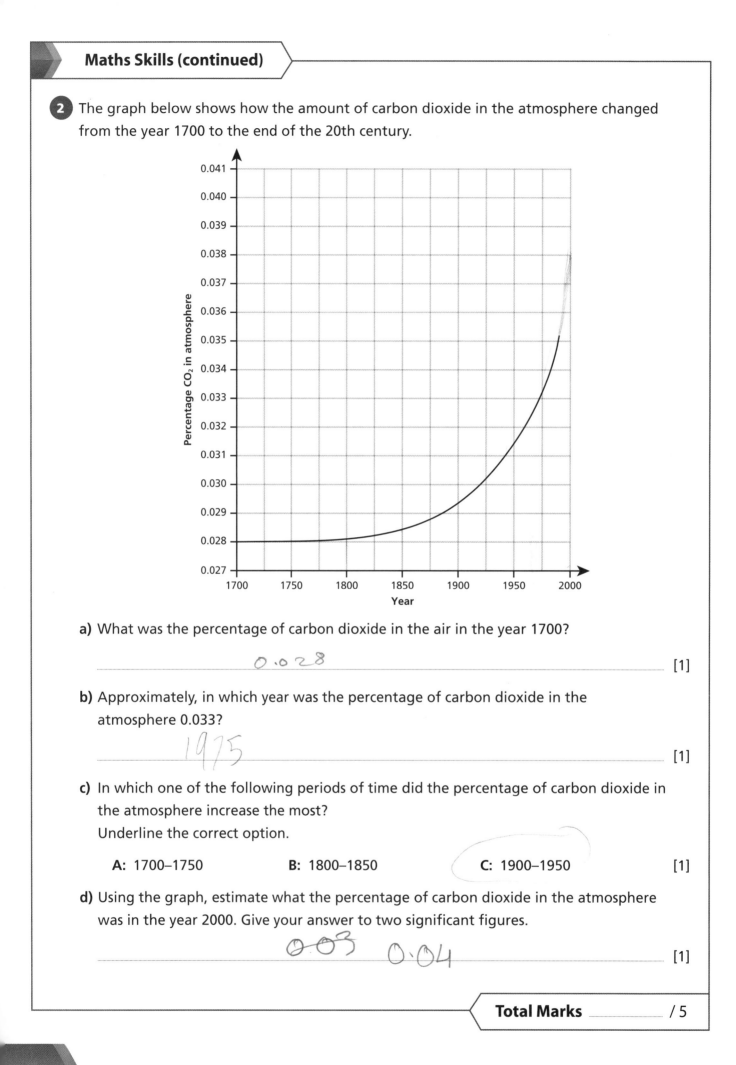

a) What was the percentage of carbon dioxide in the air in the year 1700?

0.028 [1]

b) Approximately, in which year was the percentage of carbon dioxide in the atmosphere 0.033?

1975 [1]

c) In which one of the following periods of time did the percentage of carbon dioxide in the atmosphere increase the most?
Underline the correct option.

A: 1700–1750   B: 1800–1850   C: 1900–1950 [1]

d) Using the graph, estimate what the percentage of carbon dioxide in the atmosphere was in the year 2000. Give your answer to two significant figures.

0.03 0.04 [1]

Total Marks _____ / 5

1 Underline the type of rock in which you are most likely to find examples of fossils.

    A: Igneous   **B:** Sedimentary   **C:** Metamorphic   [1]

2 Which one of the following processes does **not** release carbon dioxide into the atmosphere? Underline the correct option.

    A: Photosynthesis   **B:** Respiration   **C:** Combustion   [1]

3 Which of the following statements about rocks are true (**T**) and which are false (**F**)? Write **T** or **F** in the spaces provided.

    a) Igneous rocks are formed from cooling lava and magma.   [1]

    b) Sedimentary rocks are frequently found in layers.   [1]

    c) Large crystals in igneous rocks indicate that the rocks cooled quickly.   [1]

    d) Sedimentary rocks are most commonly formed under the sea.   [1]

4 The diagram below shows the structure of the Earth.
Correctly label each layer using the terms in the box.

inner core	outer core	crust	mantle

A: ....

B: ....

C: ....

D: ....

    [3]

5 Suggest two reasons why we are encouraged to recycle everyday materials such as paper, glass and aluminium.

....

....   [2]

6 The diagram below shows the carbon cycle.

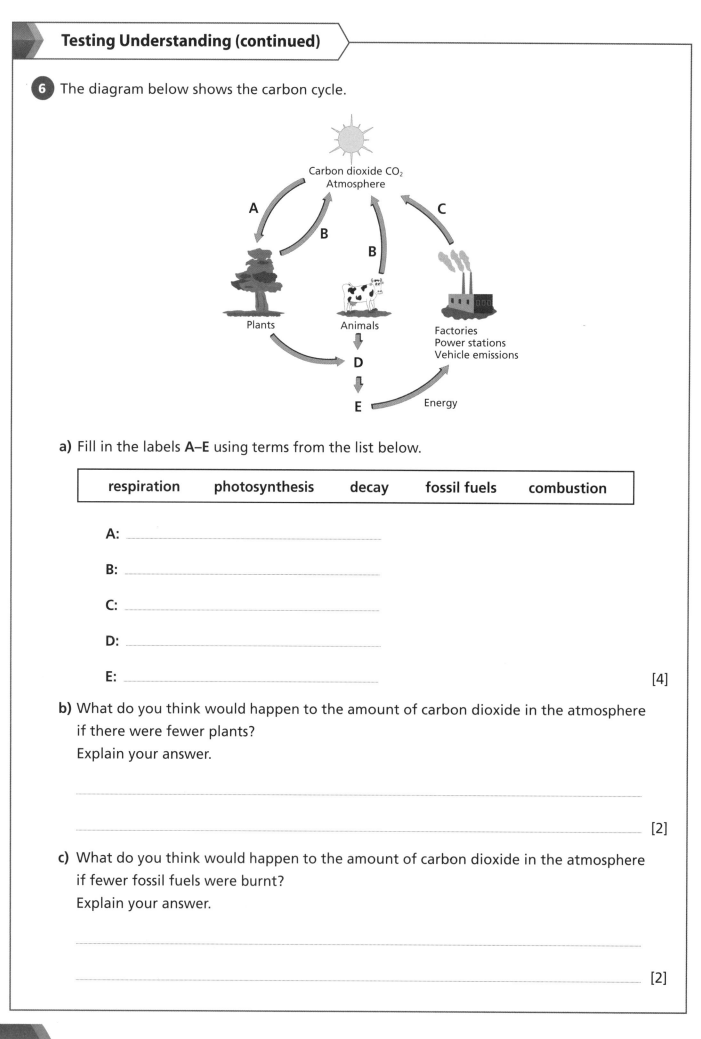

a) Fill in the labels **A–E** using terms from the list below.

respiration	photosynthesis	decay	fossil fuels	combustion

A: ....

B: ....

C: ....

D: ....

E: .... [4]

b) What do you think would happen to the amount of carbon dioxide in the atmosphere
if there were fewer plants?
Explain your answer.

....

.... [2]

c) What do you think would happen to the amount of carbon dioxide in the atmosphere
if fewer fossil fuels were burnt?
Explain your answer.

....

.... [2]

7 The diagram below shows the rock cycle.

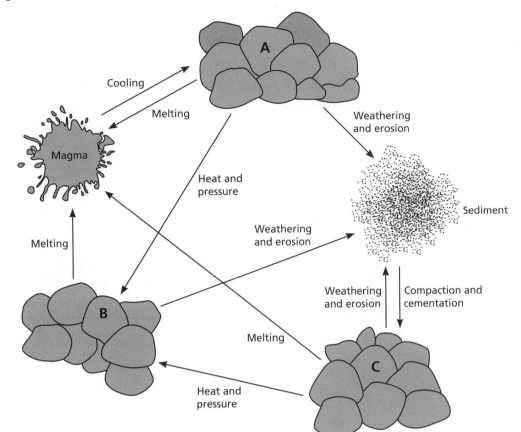

a) For the rocks in the diagram, identify which is **igneous**, which is **sedimentary** and which is **metamorphic**.

A: ....

B: ....

C: ....   [2]

b) i) What is **weathering**?

.... [1]

ii) Give one example of a type of weathering.

.... [1]

c) State one way in which magma is released onto the Earth's surface.

.... [1]

8 Look at the two pictures below. They show the crystal sizes in two different rocks.

Rock A   Rock B

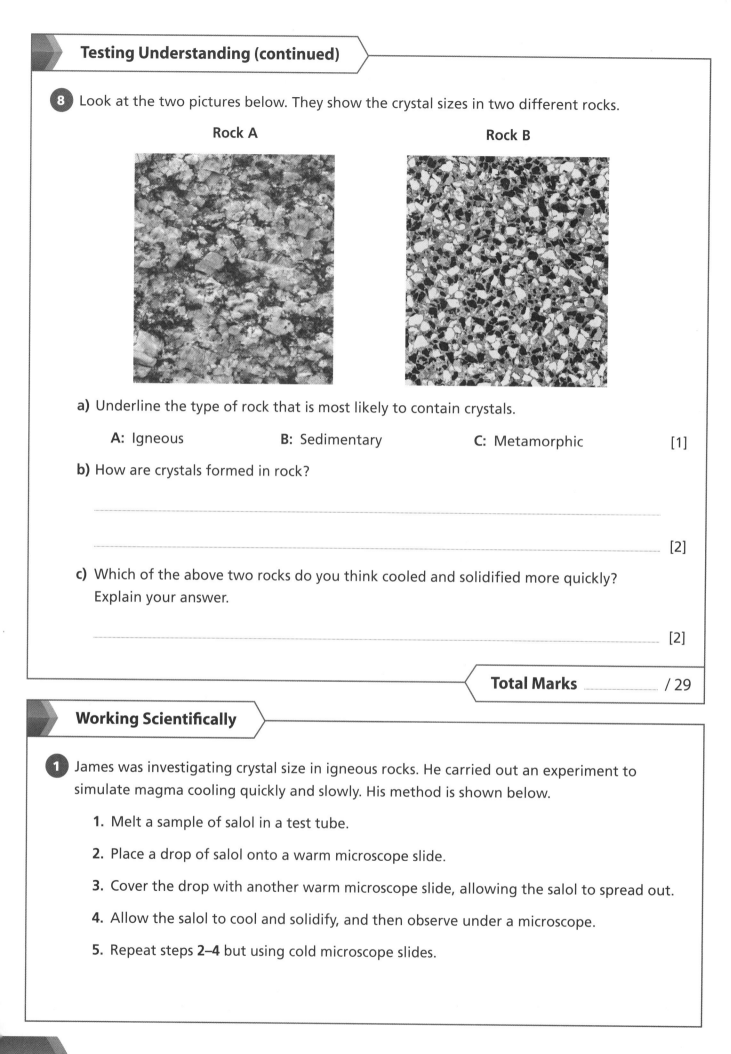

a) Underline the type of rock that is most likely to contain crystals.

   A: Igneous   **B:** Sedimentary   **C:** Metamorphic   [1]

b) How are crystals formed in rock?

   ....

   .... [2]

c) Which of the above two rocks do you think cooled and solidified more quickly?
   Explain your answer.

   .... [2]

Total Marks .... / 29

Working Scientifically

1 James was investigating crystal size in igneous rocks. He carried out an experiment to simulate magma cooling quickly and slowly. His method is shown below.

   1. Melt a sample of salol in a test tube.

   2. Place a drop of salol onto a warm microscope slide.

   3. Cover the drop with another warm microscope slide, allowing the salol to spread out.

   4. Allow the salol to cool and solidify, and then observe under a microscope.

   5. Repeat steps **2–4** but using cold microscope slides.

a) In James's experiment, what was simulating the magma?
Explain your answer.

....

.... [2]

b) How was James able to change the rate at which the salol solidified?

.... [1]

c) What is the **independent** variable in this experiment?

.... [1]

d) What is the **dependent** variable in this experiment?

.... [1]

e) James drew diagrams of the crystals he observed when the salol had cooled and solidified. The diagram on the left shows the size of some of the crystals formed on the warm microscope slides.

In the circle on the right, sketch a diagram to show the crystal size that would have been formed on the cold microscope slides.

**Crystals Formed
on Warm Slides**

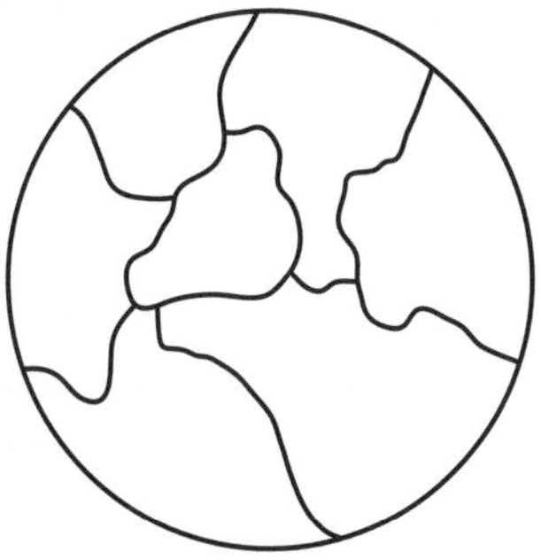

**Crystals Formed
on Cold Slides**

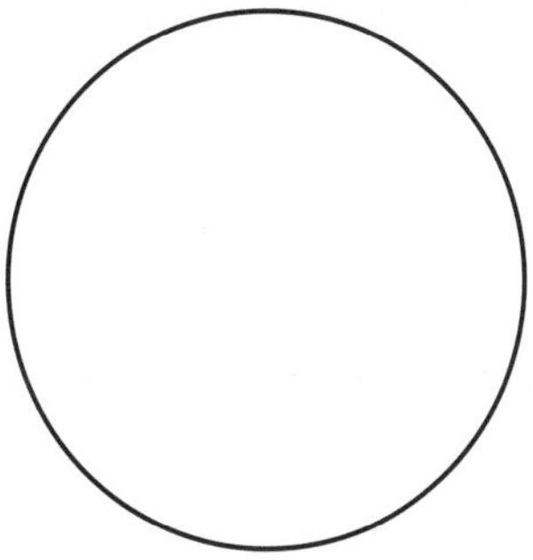

[1]

f) Does **intrusive** or **extrusive** igneous rock have larger crystals?
Explain your answer.

....

....

.... [2]

1 Read the passage below about the destruction of the rainforests and then answer the questions that follow.

The rainforests, such as those in Brazil, are described by many people as **the Earth's lungs**. Some estimates suggest that humans are cutting down an area the size of a football pitch at a rate of more than one per second. This is done to **produce wood**, either to burn or for use in the manufacture of furniture, as well as to **clear land** for growing crops, grazing cattle or as an area for people to live.

Deforestation in the Amazon Rainforest

Chemists have devised techniques such as **carbon capture and storage (CCS)** to try to reduce the amount of carbon dioxide in the atmosphere. One technique involves collecting waste gases, separating the carbon dioxide and storing it underground (for example, in old oil fields).

a) What do you think is meant by the term **the Earth's lungs**?
   Explain your answer.

   _____

   _____

   _____ [2]

b) What effect does deforestation have on carbon dioxide levels in the atmosphere?
   Explain your answer.

   _____

   _____

   _____

   _____ [2]

c) Why are scientists concerned about the level of carbon dioxide in the atmosphere?

   _____

   _____

   _____ [2]

d) Suggest reasons why carbon capture and storage is an expensive process.

....

....

....

.... [3]

2 Read the passage below about acid rain and then answer the questions that follow.

In the atmosphere many gases, such as **sulfur dioxide**, **oxides of nitrogen** and **carbon dioxide**, **dissolve in water** forming an **acidic solution**. This is how acid rain is formed.

Acid rain can damage buildings made out of certain rocks, as shown in this photo of a statue.

a) Give two ways that human activity increases the amount of carbon dioxide in the atmosphere.

....

.... [2]

b) Give two ways in which carbon dioxide is removed from the atmosphere.

....

.... [2]

c) Name an environmental problem, other than acid rain, for which carbon dioxide in the atmosphere is a contributing factor.

.... [1]

Total Marks .... / 14

	Vocabulary Builder	Maths Skills	Testing Understanding	Working Scientifically	Science in Use
Total Marks	.... / 13	.... / 5	.... / 29	.... / 8	.... / 14

Vocabulary Builder

1 Complete the passage below by filling in the gaps with key words from the box.

upwards	gravity	electricity
downwards	weight	momentum

Every object on the Earth has a mass. A force due to _____ acts on each

mass to give each object a _____. This force acts in a _____

direction towards the centre of the Earth. [3]

2 Complete the following passage about the Sun's structure by circling the correct words in bold.

The Sun is the closest **planet / moon / star** to the Earth. The Sun uses up its mass at a rate of 4 million tonnes every second through nuclear **fusion / fission**. During this process, **hydrogen / helium / oxygen** atoms join to make **carbon / helium / neon** atoms. When the Sun runs out of its primary energy source, it will expand massively to become a **neutron star / black hole / red giant**. [5]

3 Place the following key words in order of size starting from the Earth's Moon. Write the letters **A–E** in the spaces provided.

A: universe	B: star	C: planet	D: galaxy	E: solar system

Moon → _____ → _____ → _____ → _____ → _____ [1]

4 Complete the following sentences by filling in the gaps with key words.

The Earth moves around the Sun in a near circular _____ that is

called an _____.

To complete one revolution, it takes about one _____.

The Earth and Sun are kept in this arrangement by the _____ force between

the Earth's mass and the Sun's mass. [4]

5 Astronomers often use the light year when describing astronomical objects.
Define what is meant by a **light year**.

....

.... [2]

6 What is the difference between **mass** and **weight**?
Give the units of both.

....

....

....

.... [5]

Total Marks .... / 20

Maths Skills

1 An astronaut has a mass of 72kg.
The strength of the gravitational field on Earth is approximately 10N/kg.

a) What is the astronaut's weight on Earth?

....

.... [2]

b) What is the astronaut's weight if they land on Mars?
(Gravitational field strength on Mars is 3.7N/kg.)

....

.... [2]

2 Light travels at 300 000 000m/s.
Calculate how long it takes for the Sun's rays to reach the Earth if the distance between the Sun and the Earth is 150 000 000km.
Give your answer to the nearest minute.

....

....

.... [3]

3 The nearest star outside our Solar System is Alpha Centauri. It is some 3.7 light years from Earth.

a) How long does it take light from Alpha Centauri to reach the Earth?

_____ [1]

b) If light travels at 300 000 000m/s, determine how far away Alpha Centauri is from Earth. Give your answer in kilometres (to 2 s.f.).
(Use 1 year = 31 600 000 seconds.)

_____

_____

_____ [3]

4 In a cycling race, cyclist A passes a checkpoint at a speed of 15m/s at the same time as cyclist B, who is travelling at a speed of 10m/s.
40m after the checkpoint, cyclist A passes a stationary cyclist (cyclist C) who has a puncture.

On the grid below, plot a distance–time graph for all three cyclists.
Clearly label your graph to indicate each cyclist.

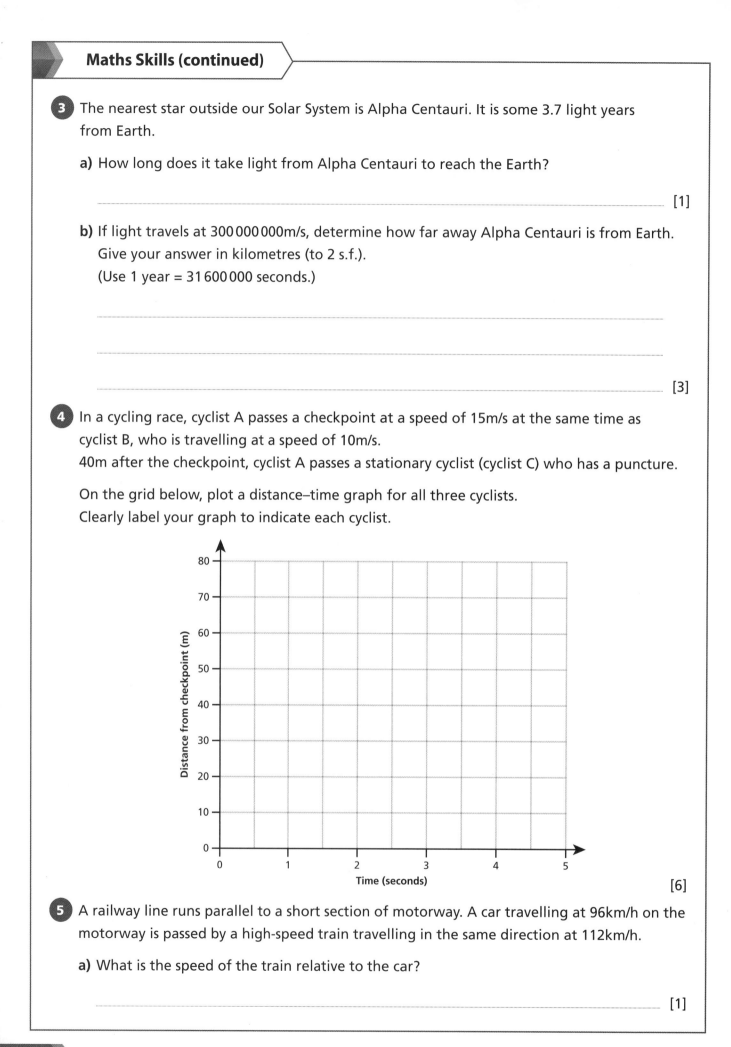

[6]

5 A railway line runs parallel to a short section of motorway. A car travelling at 96km/h on the motorway is passed by a high-speed train travelling in the same direction at 112km/h.

a) What is the speed of the train relative to the car?

_____ [1]

b) What is the speed of the car relative to the train?

.... [2]

c) If the train was travelling in the opposite direction to the car, what would be the speed of the train relative to the car?

.... [2]

Total Marks .... / 22

1 Look at the following diagram and the position of the UK (indicated).

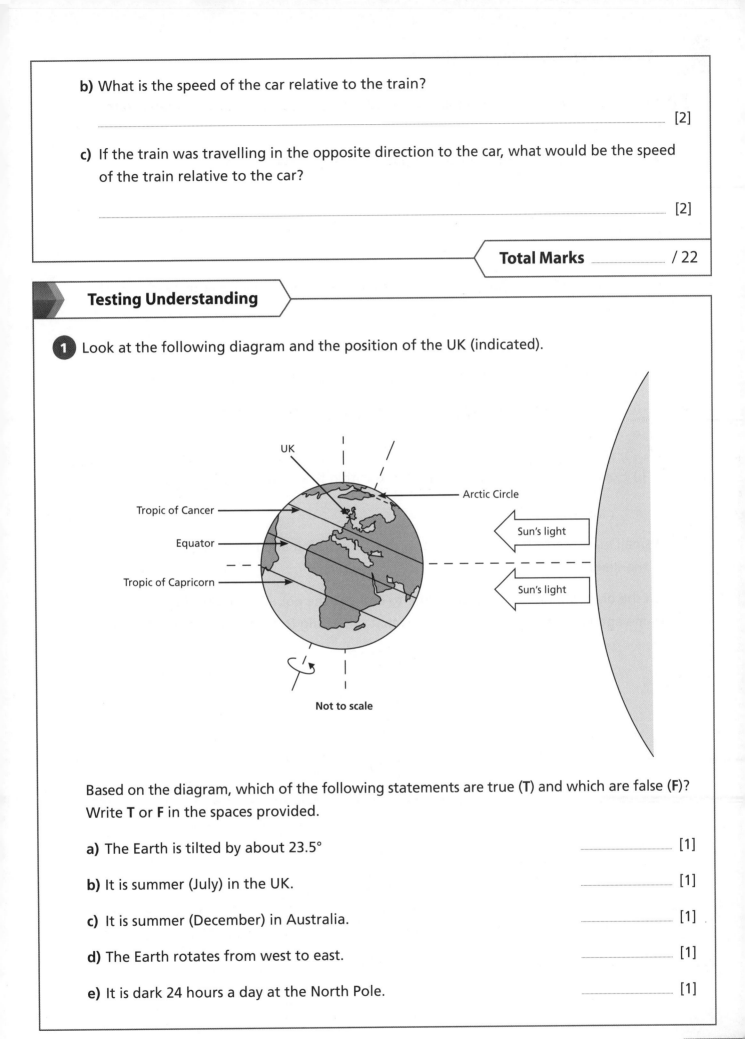

Not to scale

Based on the diagram, which of the following statements are true (**T**) and which are false (**F**)? Write **T** or **F** in the spaces provided.

a) The Earth is tilted by about 23.5° .... [1]

b) It is summer (July) in the UK. .... [1]

c) It is summer (December) in Australia. .... [1]

d) The Earth rotates from west to east. .... [1]

e) It is dark 24 hours a day at the North Pole. .... [1]

2 The following questions are about the length of a day on Earth (you may refer to the diagram on page 53).

a) The length of a day depends on the latitude of the location.
What is meant by the term **latitude**?

....

.... [2]

b) Approximately how many hours of sunshine are there on the equator every day of the year?

.... [1]

c) On 21st June (the summer solstice), the North Pole is tilted towards the Sun.

i) How many hours of daylight are there on the tropic of Cancer?

.... [1]

ii) How many hours of daylight are there within the Arctic Circle?

.... [1]

3 A small mass is attached to the end of a thin steel spring and rests in equilibrium, as shown in the diagram.

On the diagram, draw a horizontal line to indicate the equilibrium position.
Name and label the two principal forces that are acting from the equilibrium position.

[4]

4 A large box is lying stationary on a rough floor.
The box is in equilibrium.

On the diagram, draw and label the four key forces (**weight**, **pull**, **friction** and **reaction**) that are involved in maintaining this equilibrium position.

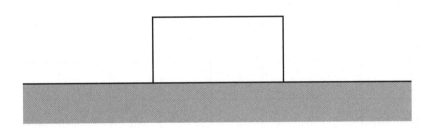

[4]

5 Read the following statements and fill in the correct names of the forces involved to maintain equilibrium.

a) A skydiver reaches terminal velocity and travels at a constant speed.

Force 1 .... = Force 2 .... [1]

b) A mass is attached at the end of a spring.

Force 1 .... = Force 2 .... [1]

c) A book is lying on a horizontal table; it is not moving.

Force 1 .... = Force 2 .... [1]

d) An aeroplane is flying horizontally at a constant speed.

i) Force 1 .... = Force 2 .... [1]

ii) Force 3 .... = Force 4 .... [1]

Total Marks .... / 23

1 A class conducts an experiment to test the bending properties of a plastic metre ruler. The apparatus is set up as shown, with weights attached to the centre of the ruler.

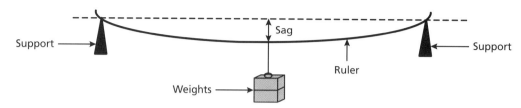

The amount of distortion, or sagging, is recorded after each weight is attached and removed. The results are shown in the table.

Mass (kg)	0.1	0.2	0.3	0.4	0.5	0.6	0.7	0.8	0.9	1.0
Load (N)										
Sag (mm)	3.5	7	10.5	14	17.5	21	24.5	28	31.5	–

a) Complete the table by determining the load values used in the experiment.
(Use g = 10N/kg.)   [2]

b) i) Plot the points on the graph below, to show the load versus the amount of sag.

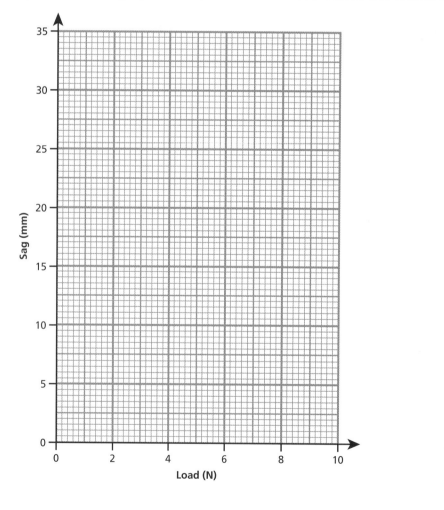

[2]

ii) Draw the line of best fit through the points and hence determine the gradient of the line (to 2 s.f.).

Give the units for the gradient.

_____

_____

_____ [3]

c) Comment on what this might suggest about the behaviour of the ruler.

_____ [1]

d) Suggest why there is no result given when a mass of 1kg is attached to the ruler.

_____ [1]

e) i) Use your graph to predict what load would be needed to give a sag of 16mm. _____ [1]

ii) Use your graph to predict what sag would be produced if weights with a total mass of 0.85kg were attached to the ruler. _____ [1]

f) i) When a load is attached, a downward force is produced but the ruler remains in equilibrium.

Where does the balancing upward force come from?

_____ [1]

ii) What happens to this upward force when larger masses are attached to the ruler?

_____ [1]

g) i) What would you expect the effect to be if two plastic rulers were used on top of each other instead of one?

_____ [1]

ii) How would this affect the results?

_____ [1]

h) What scientific method can be adopted to verify that these results are accurate?

_____ [1]

Total Marks _____ / 16

1 Read the passage below about gravitational attraction and then answer the questions that follow.

The idea that every planet in the Solar System has a **gravitational field** is very important. It reveals information about the **structure of the planet** even though it may not have been visited by a spacecraft.

The graph below shows a plot of the strength of the gravitational field on the surface of a planet versus the planet's data concerning its mass and radius. This is given by the **mass–radius index**, which is given by the expression:

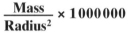

$$\frac{\text{Mass}}{\text{Radius}^2} \times 1\,000\,000$$

where the radius is in kilometres and the mass is given relative to the Earth's mass (taken to be 1000).

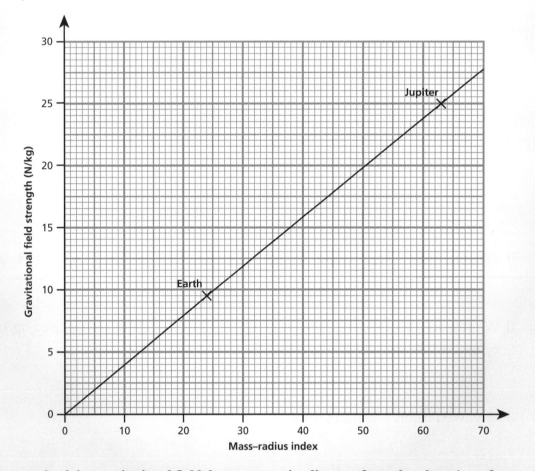

The strength of the **gravitational field decreases** as the **distance from the planet's surface increases**, but it never disappears altogether as there is always a gravitational attraction between any two masses, however small. This means that throughout the Solar System each planet, moon, asteroid and the Sun all contribute to the gravitational attraction of a spacecraft that is travelling through space. Fortunately, these forces are small. The connection between the mass, radius (and, hence, density) of a planet and its gravitational field allows the properties of other astronomical bodies in the Solar System (e.g. moons, asteroids, comets) to be determined.

a) What two important physical properties does the gravitational field strength depend on?

_____ and _____ [2]

b) What happens to the strength of the gravitational field if:

  i) the mass increases (but the radius remains the same)

  _____ [1]

  ii) the radius increases (but the mass remains the same)?

  _____ [1]

c) Neptune is the furthest planet from the Sun, with a mean radius of 22 300km.
It has a mass of 17 200, compared with 1000 for the Earth (i.e. its mass is 17.2 times larger than the Earth's).

  i) Calculate the value of the mass–radius index for Neptune (to 2 s.f.).

  _____

  _____

  _____

  _____ [3]

  ii) Using your answer to part **i)** and the graph on page 58, determine the gravitational field strength on Neptune.

  _____

  _____ [1]

d) Io is one of the largest moons around Jupiter with a mass of only 15 compared to the Earth (1000).
From satellite data, Io has a gravitational field strength of 4.5N/kg.

  i) Use the graph to determine the value of the mass–radius index for Io.

  _____

  _____ [1]

ii) Using your answer to part **i)**, show that the radius of Io is approximately 1100km.

$$\left(\text{Use Radius}^2 = \frac{\text{Mass} \times 1\,000\,000}{\text{Mass–Radius Index}}.\right)$$

[4]

e) The largest body in the Solar System is the Sun. Its mass is huge but so is its size.

i) Use the information in the table below to calculate the Sun's mass–radius index value (to 3 s.f.).

Mass (Earth = 1000)	Radius (km)
333 000 000	696 000

[3]

ii) Using your answer to part **i)** and information gathered indirectly from the graph on page 58, determine an approximate value for the Sun's gravitational field strength (to 2 s.f.).

[2]

Total Marks _____ / 18

	Vocabulary Builder	Maths Skills	Testing Understanding	Working Scientifically	Science in Use
Total Marks	/ 20	/ 22	/ 23	/ 16	/ 18

Physics

Waves and Energy Transfer

Vocabulary Builder

1 Explain what is meant by **wave superposition**.

....

....

....

.... [4]

2 Place each of the following properties in the correct column in the table.

electromagnetic	mechanical	longitudinal	transverse
300 000 000m/s	330m/s	can travel through a vacuum	needs a medium

Sound Waves	Light Waves

[4]

3 When light rays pass through a material they may cast a shadow.
Draw lines to match each statement to the appropriate key word.

Statement	Key Word
Casts no shadow	Translucent
Casts a weak shadow	Opaque
Casts a strong shadow	Transparent

[2]

4 Explain the difference between **heat** and **temperature**.

.... [2]

5 Explain the difference between **diffuse scattering** and **specular reflection**.

Diffuse scattering: ....

.... [2]

Specular reflection: ....

.... [2]

6 Which of the following statements about light moving from air to glass are true (**T**) and which are false (**F**)? Write **T** or **F** in the spaces provided.

a) Light rays speed up on entering glass. .... [1]

b) Light rays are refracted when they change speed and direction
   when entering glass. .... [1]

c) Glass is optically denser than air. .... [1]

7 Give the two key statements involved in defining the law of **Conservation of Energy**.

....

....

....

.... [2]

8 a) Describe how **photochemical smog** is formed.

....

.... [3]

b) Write down the reactants and the products of a photochemical reaction.

.... + ... → .... + ... [4]

9 Complete the following statements by filling in each gap with the correct name.

a) Energy is transferred through a material by .... [1]

b) Sunlight entering and leaving raindrops produces a .... [1]

c) White light is split up in a prism by the process of .... [1]

d) The distance between two successive crests of a wave is called its .... [1]

e) The lens in an eye is a .... lens. [1]

Total Marks .... / 33

1 In an experiment, 0.3kg of water is heated from 20°C to 50°C.

The energy transferred to the water is given by the equation:

Energy transfer (J) = Mass of water (kg) × 4200 × Change in temperature (°C)

Use this equation to determine the amount of energy transferred to the water, given the conditions above.

Give your answer in kilojoules (to 2 s.f.).

[4]

2 Convert the following into the units specified.

a) 2.15kW into joules per second

[2]

b) 6 350 000 joules into MJ

[1]

c) 8 460 000 joules into kWh
(1kWh = 3600kJ)

[3]

3 A 40W light bulb was left on for 8 hours.
Calculate the amount of energy transferred.
Give your answer in megajoules (to 2 s.f.).

[4]

4) A kettle containing 0.35 litres of water is heated from 20°C to the boiling point of water.
If 4200 joules of energy are transferred when the temperature of 1 litre of water is raised by
1°C, determine the total amount of energy transferred in boiling the water.
Give your answer in kilojoules (to 2 s.f.).

[4]

5) A small semi-detached house receives a bill for its monthly usage of gas (650kWh) and
electricity (400kWh).
If the cost of gas is £0.04 per kWh and the cost of electricity is £0.13 per kWh, what is the
total monthly bill for the energy used?

[5]

6) The nutritional information on a tin of sardines gives the energy per can as 779kJ.
Calculate the energy equivalent in terms of kilocalories, giving your answer to the nearest
kilocalorie. (1kJ = 0.240kcal)

[3]

Total Marks _____ / 26

Testing Understanding

1) Explain the key difference between an **insulator** and a **conductor** in terms of
energy transfer.

Insulator: _____

[1]

Conductor: _____

[1]

2 The diagram shows an object (a candle) and an eye.
On the diagram, draw two light rays from the object to show how the image of the candle is produced on the back of the eye.

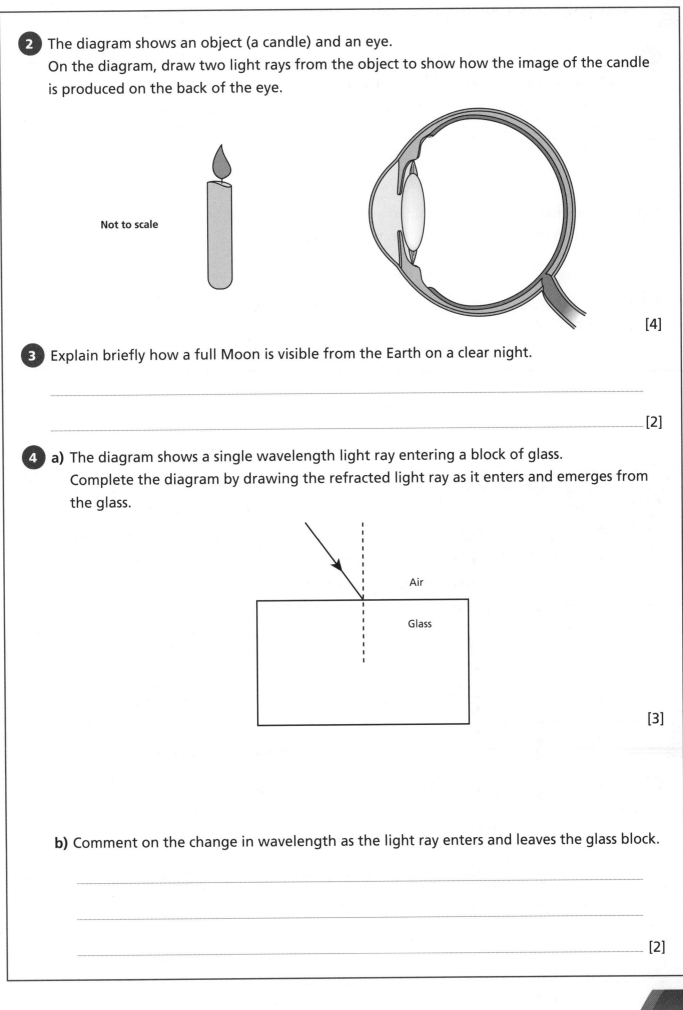

Not to scale

[4]

3 Explain briefly how a full Moon is visible from the Earth on a clear night.

....

....[2]

4 **a)** The diagram shows a single wavelength light ray entering a block of glass.
Complete the diagram by drawing the refracted light ray as it enters and emerges from the glass.

Air

Glass

[3]

b) Comment on the change in wavelength as the light ray enters and leaves the glass block.

....

....

....[2]

5 If four complete waves pass through a particular point every second, what is the frequency of the wave? Give the units of frequency.

[2]

6 Describe three ways in which energy is stored.

[3]

7 Describe what happens to the end of a metal rod when the other end is heated. Your explanation should be based on the particle model.

[5]

Total Marks .... / 23

Working Scientifically

1 An investigation was carried out looking at the way hot coffee cools in a paper coffee cup with and without a plastic lid. The coffee was heated to an initial temperature of 93°C and left to cool in its natural surroundings on top of a bench. The temperature was recorded every minute and the results are shown below. The temperature in the laboratory was 20°C.

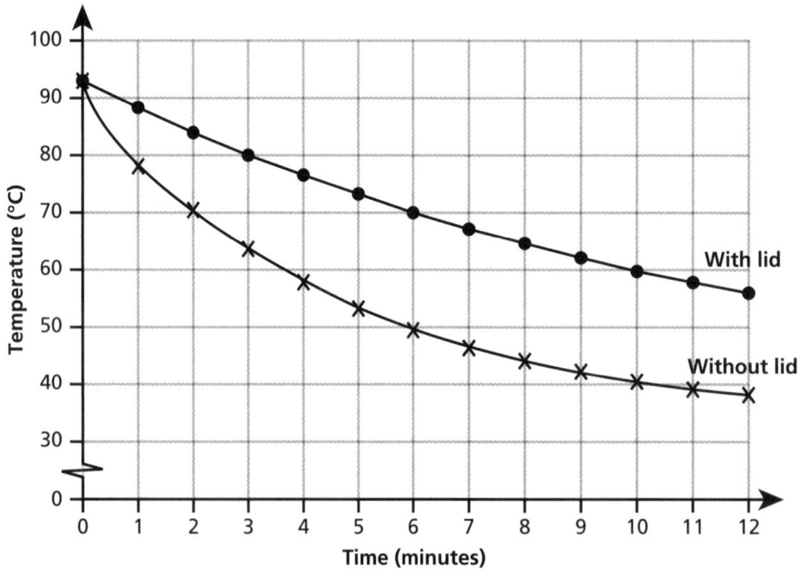

a) Describe what happens to the coffee in each experimental situation.

With lid: _____

_____ [2]

Without lid: _____

_____ [3]

b) What would be the final temperature of the coffee in both experiments?

_____ [1]

c) The ideal drinking temperature is around 60°C.
Estimate how long it takes the coffee to cool to this temperature in each experiment.

With lid: _____ [1]

Without lid: _____ [1]

d) Estimate the rate of cooling in each experiment after 4 minutes.
Use the data at 3 and 5 minutes to give the temperature drop in 2 minutes to help you.
Give your answers in degrees Celsius per minute.

With lid: _____

_____ [2]

Without lid: _____

_____ [2]

e) Explain how heat is lost from the cup of coffee.

_____

_____

_____

_____ [5]

f) What conclusions can you draw from this experiment?

_____

_____ [2]

Total Marks _____ / 19

1 Read the following passage and then answer the questions that follow.

The human body needs **energy** in the form of **food** in order to function and do work internally and externally. When food is consumed, energy within the food is transferred into chemical energy in the body, which in turn is transported to the areas that require an energy source.

The energy requirement per second to keep the body functioning when resting (i.e. sleeping) is called the **Basal Metabolic Rate (BMR)**. In these circumstances, the release of energy is small but enough to keep the body's vital organs, such as the heart, lungs and brain, functioning. For an average adult, the BMR is between 60W and 80W, although the precise amount depends on a number of factors, such as body size.

When the body is undertaking additional activity, extra energy is required. The table below shows typical rates of energy conversion for various activities.

Activity	Rate of Energy Conversion (W)
Sleeping	80
Walking	250
Jogging	400
Swimming	500

Clearly an adequate intake of food is necessary in order to carry out these activities. The amount of energy contained in food is given as **nutritional information** on product packaging, often expressed in units of kilojoules or kilocalories per 100g or per individual portion. The conversion used is **1kJ = 0.240kcal**.

a) Determine the amount of energy required by an adult when sleeping for 8 hours. Give your answer in kcal (to 2 s.f.).

[5]

b) Nyoko takes her morning exercise in a gym, which involves jogging for 20 minutes and swimming for 15 minutes. Her BMR is 60W.

Determine the total amount of energy Nyoko expends in doing these exercises.

Give your answer in kcal (to 2 s.f.).

[5]

c) The following nutritional information appears on a 60g energy bar.

Nutritional Information		
Typical Values	Per 60g Bar (kJ / kcal)	Per 100g (kJ / kcal)
Energy	890 / 214	1483 / 356
Protein (g)	2	4
Carbohydrate (g)	44	72
of which sugars (g)	23	39
of which fructose (g)	12	20
Fat (g)	3.3	5.6
of which saturates (g)	0.5	0.8
Others	10.7	18.4

i) Would one energy bar be sufficient to replenish the energy Nyoko uses in her morning exercise routine?
Explain your answer.

....

....

....

.... [2]

ii) What assumption have you made in determining your answer to part **i)**?

....

.... [1]

d) Nyoko exercises with her friend Jasmine, who has a much greater BMR than Nyoko.
How does Jasmine's required energy intake compare to Nyoko's?

.... [1]

e) A lot of energy is stored as sugar.
How much energy is stored in the sugar component of the energy bar?
Give your answer in kcal (to 2 s.f.).

....

....

....

....

.... [4]

f) Nyoko is planning to run a half-marathon, which she hopes to complete in around 3 hours.
Estimate the amount of energy Nyoko needs to achieve this.
Give your answer in kcal (to 2 s.f.).

....

....

....

.... [3]

Total Marks .... / 21

	Vocabulary Builder	Maths Skills	Testing Understanding	Working Scientifically	Science in Use
Total Marks	.... / 33	.... / 26	.... / 23	.... / 19	.... / 21

Notes

The Periodic Table

Key

relative atomic mass
atomic symbol
name
atomic (proton) number

1		2												3	4	5	6	7	0
							1 **H** hydrogen 1												4 **He** helium 2
7 **Li** lithium 3		9 **Be** beryllium 4												11 **B** boron 5	12 **C** carbon 6	14 **N** nitrogen 7	16 **O** oxygen 8	19 **F** fluorine 9	20 **Ne** neon 10
23 **Na** sodium 11		24 **Mg** magnesium 12												27 **Al** aluminium 13	28 **Si** silicon 14	31 **P** phosphorus 15	32 **S** sulfur 16	35.5 **Cl** chlorine 17	40 **Ar** argon 18
39 **K** potassium 19		40 **Ca** calcium 20	45 **Sc** scandium 21	48 **Ti** titanium 22	51 **V** vanadium 23	52 **Cr** chromium 24	55 **Mn** manganese 25	56 **Fe** iron 26	59 **Co** cobalt 27	59 **Ni** nickel 28	63.5 **Cu** copper 29	65 **Zn** zinc 30		70 **Ga** gallium 31	73 **Ge** germanium 32	75 **As** arsenic 33	79 **Se** selenium 34	80 **Br** bromine 35	84 **Kr** krypton 36
85 **Rb** rubidium 37		88 **Sr** strontium 38	89 **Y** yttrium 39	91 **Zr** zirconium 40	93 **Nb** niobium 41	96 **Mo** molybdenum 42	[98] **Tc** technetium 43	101 **Ru** ruthenium 44	103 **Rh** rhodium 45	106 **Pd** palladium 46	108 **Ag** silver 47	112 **Cd** cadmium 48		115 **In** indium 49	119 **Sn** tin 50	122 **Sb** antimony 51	128 **Te** tellurium 52	127 **I** iodine 53	131 **Xe** xenon 54
133 **Cs** caesium 55		137 **Ba** barium 56	139 **La*** lanthanum 57	178 **Hf** hafnium 72	181 **Ta** tantalum 73	184 **W** tungsten 74	186 **Re** rhenium 75	190 **Os** osmium 76	192 **Ir** iridium 77	195 **Pt** platinum 78	197 **Au** gold 79	201 **Hg** mercury 80		204 **Tl** thallium 81	207 **Pb** lead 82	209 **Bi** bismuth 83	[209] **Po** polonium 84	[210] **At** astatine 85	[222] **Rn** radon 86
[223] **Fr** francium 87		[226] **Ra** radium 88	[227] **Ac*** actinium 89	[261] **Rf** rutherfordium 104	[262] **Db** dubnium 105	[266] **Sg** seaborgium 106	[264] **Bh** bohrium 107	[277] **Hs** hassium 108	[268] **Mt** meitnerium 109	[271] **Ds** darmstadtium 110	[272] **Rg** roentgenium 111								

Elements with atomic numbers 112–116 have been reported but not fully authenticated

*The Lanthanoids (atomic numbers 58–71) and the Actinoids (atomic numbers 90–103) have been omitted.

Cu and **Cl** have not been rounded to the nearest whole number.